My Life
What a Life

THIRD EDITION

You must prepare yourself to reach your dream.

MIGUEL A. PINZÓN, Ph.D.

Proceeds from this book aid students in
need of financial assistance to attend college.

ISBN: 1453642439
ISBN 13: 9781453642436

Pinzón's debut memoir details a life of epic scope—from preteen immigrant working for an Arizona rancher, to police officer, corporate sales manager, university professor, international-investment manager, and charity volunteer.

In this wide-ranging book, the author pays closest attention to his early life, charting his evolution from a member of a close-knit community to an outsider beset by bigotry. As a university student, he became politically active, advocating the commonality of all peoples. His life shifted because of events outside his control.

However, his life choices demonstrate the power of his drive and determination and highlight his unshakeable commitment to family, mentors, co-workers, and people in need. The narrative intersperses events in Pinzón's life with the various guidelines he has followed along the way, including the police officer's code of ethics and his own corporate policies.

During the business phase of his life, the narrative scales back on personal disclosures and detours into professional lessons and includes an impassioned plea for changes in corporate behavior. Here, the author provides pages of tips on starting a business and tells the success story of a self-starting teenage Nepali entrepreneur.

The memoir ends not by summing up the author's experiences, but with a call for personal responsibility and team building in all areas of life. It's a consistent and fitting conclusion to Pinzón's inspirational and instructive story.

An engaging life story that effectively demonstrates the concept that no man is an island.

Kirkus Reviews

In reading Dr. Pinzón's book I was captivated by the author's zest for life, his unwillingness to give up, and his courage in tackling new and dramatic career changes, all for one purpose--to make this a better world than the one he was born into. In that goal he has succeeded, and then some. By showing us the inherent strength of our nation's diversity, a concept that is not to be feared but indeed to be embraced, by offering solutions that have so vexed our politicians, by showing the interconnectedness of all peoples and just how interrelated our world is, Dr. Pinzón, with great humor and an unabashed love of his fellow man, illuminates a path, particularly for young people seeking fulfilment, regardless of whatever burdens they may carry. In our short time on this earth, in our mortality, it is said that everyone dies, but not everyone "lives". Dr. Pinzón has and is very much "living" a full life, of service to others and to our world. A great read.

Judge Jorge J. Perez (Retired)
Circuit Court in and for the 11th Judicial Circuit
Miami, Florida

Dedication

For Tina, my wife. Together we have created a wonderful daughter, and a love affair blessed with many-splendored things. We have worked together, as a team, in our professional careers, both academically and in business. She has been with me since the beginning; without her my life would have been catastrophic.

For Mireya Anai, my dear daughter, and Aitana, my lovely grandchild. May this work inspire you both to appreciate life and people who care for a better world! The more you enrich and improve the lives of others, the more you'll enrich and improve your own.

And to those who believe and promote social change and stand together to repress corruption and racism. . .

Acknowledgments

I have been blessed with generous information from countless entrepreneurs and friends around the world, such as Prof. José Manuel Sáiz Alvarez, Nebrija University, Spain; Marc Gidney, George Lopez, Miami Beach, and Joe Bernstein, Fort Lauderdale, FL; USAF retired Col. Mike Evans, Washington, D.C.; Archbishop Alfonso Cortés, Mexico; Martha Juy, Mexico; Cardinal Timothy M. Dolan, St. Patrick's Cathedral, NY; Eric Trump, the Trump Organization, NY; Armando Lara, Oxnard, California; James Thompson from the Burj Al Arab and Ashfad in the United Arab Emirates; Theresia Anggriani from the Republic of Seychelles; Fr. Jean-Claude Hebert, Haiti; Dr. John M. Kline, Georgetown University; Lam Sau Ha, Hong Kong; Joerg Geier, the Club of Rome; multinational business managers and entrepreneurs Nari Chandiramani, Asgar S. Patel, Riya Padhye, and Preeyaa Jai Barve from India; Li Hing Chi, Hong Kong; Vijay Narsapur, DeLoitte & Touché Consulting International; Rey David, Philippines; Mark Gerber from South Africa; Stephen Zimmermann from the Inter-American Development Bank; Mireya Olivas, the World Bank; Prof. Edson Aparecida de Araujo, Brazil; Jajua Qubain from Jordan; David Swain from England; my dear late friend Count Mario Palmerino Lembo d'Aeto, Italy; Flor Ruiz from World Vision Mexico; Corina Villacorta from WV, International; Joe Bernstein, J. Ludlow and Ray, who enthusiastically worked on the manuscript; and with special gratitude for his wise advice and support, Thomas Hoffman, Manhattan.

I am indebted to my students who collaborated in researching the information in the entrepreneurship chapter in this book. Thanks to my dear friend Ann Aguilera for her constant support and inspiration; Helen Klotz, G. Brownlow, William M. Churchill, and Martin Shalenberger. Thank you to the many young people who I met throughout the Congresswoman Carolyn Maloney's 2010 re-election campaign in Manhattan and President Barak Obama's 2011-12 canvassing in Miami, who encouraged me to write my story. Also, to A. Stoudmire and B. Levin, always intrigued as to how I did it.

Without the support of all these people, and many more, this book would not have been possible. Thank you all who inspired me along the years to reach many dreams....

MAP
Sunny Isles Beach, FL

Table of Contents

Introduction

*Do not procrastinate, learn the necessary
skills and go after your dreams!*

Perhaps you are wondering why I wrote a third and final edition of this book. I chose to do so to inspire younger generations that we have to transform and get involved to make our country and the world a better place to live through our commitment, innovations, entrepreneurship, ethics, and goodwill by making a mark in our communities. If you want to succeed, take your dreams seriously. People do not succeed because they have excuses and are always blaming someone for their failures. So in order for us to reach any objective, we must face our responsibilities and be committed.

We cannot stand by watching people be unemployed, discriminated against, or not having the means with which to maintain their respect and dignity as human beings and as a family. Today we live in a tougher world, and competition is fierce. And to make matters worse, politicians and corporations are not creating new opportunities for younger generations. On the contrary, lobbyists and big corporations are slowly destroying economic progress for everyone, as a country, and worldwide—unfair wages, diminished retirement benefits, global health issues, more contaminated rivers and oceans, and the ozone problem—are provoking and environment decadence for future generations.

Although many have reached their dreams, that's not enough! We must also enjoy life by sharing our knowledge. We must ask ourselves: Are we well informed? Are we engaged in our communities? Are we involved with others, so they too can attempt to reach their dreams? Nelson Mandela properly said it that it *is humane to love and help others, so they can become productive human beings.* Life, indeed, is full of delights, challenges, responsibilities, and opportunities; and we must be ready to help, teach and motivate those who need us.

We should never forget that we are interconnected, regardless of who we are, our race, our ethnicity, or the religion we practice. In the Bible, the Prophet Ezekiel indicates that God lays upon the people the responsibility of watching out for the welfare of others. Are we, then, our brothers' keepers? Yes, we should be our brothers' keeper to a degree. We should attempt to teach and lead our fellow human beings to be responsible, and to motivate them to reach their goals. I know that this involves hard work and many frustrations. However, we also have the right to make our choices. I have attempted to do my part because I love people. I love society, and there is much more work that must be done. It is now up to you, the new generations, and the brand new generation of policy makers, to do away with negative attitudes and break from old paradigms. I am referring to people who care for other citizens and their country, and not to those who are after personal, corporate, or political party interests.

The 21st century brought many changes, and it is time to evolve into a modern social transformation; a new era and philosophy instead of remaining in the past, as Martin Luther King noted in 1967 "*...and continue to live in [several] Americas.*" Some communities "*overflowing with the milk of prosperity and the honey of opportunity,*" the others tainted by "*a daily ugliness...that constantly transforms the buoyancy of hope into the fatigue of despair.*" It is time to start working as a team, and allow justice, liberty, and opportunity to prevail for all! If we do not become one nation, we will continue to weaken our global economic and political advantage, and we could become less effective as a leading world democracy within a very short time.

In the past three decades, I have met diverse people throughout the world: indigents, wealthy people, important business and government officials, religious leaders, tribal chiefs, and European and African royalty. Regardless of their social status and culture, the majority of them had a common denominator--they expressed their anxiety about the present world situation and shared their hopes and dreams for the future. They taught me that whatever position in life we have, we should all be concerned and take responsibility for how the world operates economically, politically, and socially.

Our country and the world face very serious issues. Issues that are of particular importance to me, in regard to America, are the poverty and racial tension that have caused our democratic nation to remain divided. We live in one of the greatest countries in the world, but we must sustain it wisely if we want to have an equally great future; and to do this, we must move beyond the divisions that lead to each group fighting for only its particular rights. We are all Americans and must defend the spirit of our Constitution and its ideals of democracy, protection, and equality under the law for all.

It is impossible to achieve forward-thinking economic goals if we think and behave as if we are alone; indeed we are not alone! We must strive for mutually constructive relationships at all levels. We must always go for win-win outcomes instead of focusing exclusively on our own needs and demands. Governments, non-governmental organizations (NGOs), entrepreneurs, multinational businesses, and the wealthy all have important roles to play because they bring citizens, customers, and communities together and assist in creating jobs, wealth, and an improved standard of living. Each is part of the solution.

Due to the many characteristics that have enabled the United States to become the world's leading power, and because of our diversity of cultures, we must remain open to everyone. To not merely survive but to excel in today's world, we must try to understand other cultures, interact intelligently and empathetically with other people, and reciprocate acts of good faith. Our educational, political, economic, and religious leaders, together with us as involved citizens, must be ready to meet the challenges we face today.

We must bring about change rapidly in our diverse society and evolve into a more modern and progressive America in the next decades. Simultaneously, we must consider what goes on in other countries and how their destinies are unquestionably intertwined with our own. To take a salient example, our borders have become a dynamic and very complex problem. Our actions in defending our borders have the potential to worsen previous problems by antagonizing other cultures and making us look xenophobic.

It is time to stop being negligent, arrogant, or simply indifferent. It is time to take action to alleviate those problems that continuously affect us as a nation and to demonstrate exactly how unwarranted the "Ugly American" stereotype prevalent around the globe is. We must work harder to make our world a better place in which to live, for ourselves and for future generations. The good news is that we have goodwill, entrepreneurs, wealth, knowledge, and technology; and we follow the rules of the game.

Our leadership has placed us where we are globally. The constant and complex challenges that we face in the world today within such diverse societies obligate us to appoint leaders with open minds, integrity, and a vision that can lead to solutions to our problems. We require leaders who can provoke within us a sense of hope for the future, the thrill of possibilities, and creative solutions. They must also be effective in the art of establishing and negotiating real and practical policies, policies that have the power to change dangerous trends such as the relaxation of corporate and personal ethics and the growing imbalance in the distribution of wealth in our society.

Life has changed indeed; and it is a completely different life from that in the 20th century. The globalization, technology, the Internet, Facebook, Google, and Twitter have changed everything—society, government, and business. The new generation employees prefer being with their families or friends and having quality time instead of working long hours in an organization, as my generation did. Many of the younger generations are not willing to make sacrifices. However, the millennial generation, globally, are discontent with the same politicians they have seen since their teen years. Citizens around the world defied dictatorial governments in the Middle East and North Africa where it was never expected to occur.

In the 21st century, business-negotiations became more difficult and countless of substitute products inundated the world markets. New paradigms developed in banking, economics, and society as a whole. Markets became unpredictable; the global economy constantly started many changes, and necessary environmental laws have also drastically affected companies worldwide. The effects of *El Niño* and *La Niña* tremendously increased costs globally as well.

Meanwhile, as these changes were going on, I faced many challenges in my own life as well as in global business, and prevailed. However, the experiences have been invaluable and have given me the insight to learn and face many endeavors with responsibility, an ethical commitment, and a strong passion to better my environment.

In writing about global markets, environments, and operations in their *International Business (15th Ed.)*, John Daniels, L. Radebaugh, and D. Sullivan (2014) say it very eloquently that *"Various reliable indicators assure us that globalization has been increasing,"* and more rapidly in the late twentieth century. *"Currently, over 20 percent of world production is sold outside its country of origin, compared to about seven percent in 1950."*

In *The Wealth of Nations* (1776), Adam Smith indicated, *"Human beings want to trade with each other..."* And today, recognized world economists firmly believe that globalization will not be stopped no matter how strong political or social forces may be against it.

The KOF Economic Institute of Switzerland recently reported that the overall degree of the globalization index trend—social, political, and economic—has been toward more globalization, rather than less. Kousez and Posner wrote explicitly in their 1993 book *Credibility*, *"...shared values are the foundation for building productive and genuine working relationships."* World leaders must make agreements and build a better relationship: *"Their efforts are not to get everyone to be in accord on everything—this goal is unrealistic, perhaps even impossible...Moreover, to achieve it would negate the advantages of diversity."* However, *"in order to take a first step, and then a second...people must agree on something."* There has to be a common denominator of understanding. *"If disagreements over fundamental values continue, the result is intense conflict, false expectations, and diminished capacity. There could be no agreement on the specifications of quality, customer service, or any guiding principle. Recognizing that we hold shared values provides us with a common language with which we can collaborate...."*

The English philosopher and statesman John Locke (1632-1704) wrote in the *Second Treatise of Government* that people do not consistently behave virtuously and rationally, but that there are occasions when they are naïve, hypocritical, irrational, contentious, bigoted, and wicked. Are we a nation of this type of people? Are we the type of people with an attitude that because we have the gold, we make the rules, without any *"benevolent capitalism"* considerations? No, we are not!

I hope that the words in these pages can provide both inspiration and practical advice. I hope that the younger generations can keep their spirit alive in spite of impossible odds. Yes, you can reach your dreams. The world needs you. Our country can't wait. However, you must be well-educated and have the skills to face global challenges, and revolutionize the economy and the corporate world; and most importantly, get engaged. You can reach agreements because you have the knowledge and nanotechnology to solve problems in ways my generation never thought of in medical science, clean energy production, clean air manufacturing, global warming, human rights, world hunger and assisting developing countries. Today we have an urgent responsibility in our societies that requires a joint venture with the private industry, non-government organizations, and government to make a long-term commitment of social-economic development and sustainability.

The globalization rapidly proliferated in the first fifteen years of the 21st century along with many changes. Studies indicate that these changes also caused bad business practices to prevail globally. Business practices within an industry or within a country moved toward illegality over time. Many corporate managers have told me that to get in the business or stay in it, I had to play by *"their rules."* However, participating in a culture of business corruption is a personal dilemma. If people get involved in corrupted business/political practices, there are a few short or mid-term winners and many long-term losers. Thus, it is best to move the business elsewhere where societies are not harmed. Ethics in global business practices must prevail in order to reach good decisions that will resolve in win-win disputes across cultural boundaries, give us profits, and social benefits globally in the long term.

Life is worth living! But that of course, it depends on each one of us. If you want to succeed in life, you have to get started and never stop. But first, believe in yourself, and trust those who work with you. You must work as a team. Take command over your destiny and sincerely pray to your God for guidance in your path through life so you can continue with your personal fulfillment in the pursuit of happiness, national greatness, and make our world a better place to live.

Believe in yourself; trust and lead those wo work with you. Get involved, and ready to face global challenges; transform yourslef in order to revolutionize social change, the economy, the corporate world, and your environment.

CHAPTER I

A Promise

Every man is said to have his peculiar ambition. Whether it be true or not, I can say, for once, that I have no other so great as that of being truly esteemed by my fellow man, by rendering myself worthy of their esteem.

A. Lincoln

There are many times when I wish politicians, non-profit organization managers, governments, and the wealthy could share in those significant moments when I have been with those who are truly needy. If they could see what I have seen, they might better understand the poverty, hunger, despair, frustration, sadness, and ignorance that millions suffer daily, whether they are in Africa, Asia, Latin America, or right here in the U.S.A. By understanding these elements that choke the human spirit, and by appreciating the enormous pool of potential productivity and intellectual ability represented by those whose current focus is primarily on survival, people of influence can do something to bring about radical social and economic change.

My tears have fallen from seeing the poor going hungry or not having enough money to pay for a doctor or medicine. At the same time, my heart rejoices when I sense the beauty of their hearts as they show their feelings for one another. Their living conditions and their lives are sometimes sad, yet there is a beauty that I see in their homes that leaves me speechless; their unity and the love they have for one another is truly amazing.

I met Martha in Mexico when she was a six-year-old child. Juanita, Martha's adopted mother, tells her story:

"My husband was coming home from work late on a rainy night, and as he walked past a trash can, he found Martha there crying, covered in an old blanket, with cardboard and trash on top of her. We called the police and they did not do anything, so we took her to the hospital. Her little body was normal, but her legs were deformed. She had miniature legs, only two inches long. My husband brought this little baby home and we adopted her, even though we already had eleven children of our own and no money. We are poor people," said Juanita. As I listened to this kind, petite, shy, thirty-four-year-old woman, her words were filled with love for her adopted daughter. "Since she has been with us, Martha has brought so much love to our family. Her brothers and sister love to take care of her."

Martha was an outpatient three times a week at the *Centro de Rehabilitación Infantil* (Children's Rehabilitation Center), where I was a volunteer assisting children suffering from epilepsy and muscular dystrophy in Cuernavaca—a place known worldwide and called by Alexander von Humboldt as "the city of eternal spring." This place has such a wonderful climate that Hernán Cortés, the Spanish conquistador, built his palace there in 1526. Austrian, Maximillian I, the second emperor of Mexico, and his wife Carlota also enjoyed their residence and the city's ideal climate during his reign from 1864-1867. Woolworth heiress Barbara Hutton had her home near the city; the deposed Mohammad Reza Pahlavie, the last Shah of Iran, also established his home there in the late

1970s; and so have many well-known American politicians. English, Italian, and Russian royalty, painters such as Diego Rivera and Freida Kalho, and gangsters like Al Capone and Bugsy Siegel, actresses Rita Hayworth and Helen Hayes, and Erich Fromm and other famous novelists have lived there. Located sixty miles southwest of Mexico City, Cuernavaca is a beautiful place with a picturesque landscape accented by many colorful bougainvilleas. If you ever want to enjoy an ideal climate and taste exquisite food, visit Cuernavaca and stop by the famed restaurant *Las Mañanitas*, where many prestigious people have dined since the mid-1950s. Among the many celebrity guests was Johnny Weissmuller, star of Tarzan, who often visited when he lived in Acapulco during the last years of his life. Along with the fabulous climate of Cuernavaca, there is the spectacular view of two major volcanoes, *Popocatepetl* and *Iztaccíhuatl*. This scenery makes the town more picturesque, along with the beautiful *Santa María Asunción* Cathedral (1529-1552) with its early 17th century frescoes on the lateral walls and Diego Rivera's spectacular murals (1929-30) on the walls of an inner court at the *Palacio de Cortés*.

But I digress. Returning to the story of Martha, the chief therapist assigned little Martha to me and directed me to massage her legs so that they might gain strength. She hoped that this would help Martha be able to walk on her own later in life. I also taught Martha's mother how to give her daughter the same massage at home. It was another act of love that left me astonished--that the adopted mother of this amazing special needs child wanted to learn everything possible to help her daughter walk someday. I have seen such acts of complete unselfishness in many of the poor families' homes I have visited in many places; to experience the love and selflessness of those who have so little is truly heartwarming, to say the least.

Another family I always remember is one I met at the Rehabilitation Center. An indigent mother pleaded in her native Spanish, *"Necesito comprar jarabe para la tos que tiene mi bebé, y no tengo dinero. Podría usted ayudarme, por favor?"* Translated, "I need to buy cough syrup for my baby, and I have no money. Can you please help me?" I took a doctor to the home of this young, sad-faced woman on the outskirts of Cuernavaca. The home was made of cardboard and dirt. When the doctor examined the baby girl, he discovered bronchitis. Without medical care the child would have died within the day. A week after being treated, the baby was crying loudly and in the best of health.

A few days later, the mother walked ten miles to my pharmacy to thank me. When she saw me, she attempted to kiss my hand as a way of expressing her gratitude. I told her that I had helped her because it was the right thing to do. I told her that her thanks were sufficient. She then said, "We may not have much food or a proper home, but my husband and I have much love for our four children, and we came here to thank you. Our baby is doing well. I will always keep you in my prayers and pray to God wholeheartedly for you." She placed her hands on my head and said a prayer in Spanish mixed with her native Aztec language, *Nahuátl,* and ended by saying, "*Dios estará enternamente contigo*" (God will be with you eternally).

I have witnessed many poor families endure challenging circumstances through the years. I have visited them in their humble dwellings in many countries and have been impressed as I observed the love they had for one another. Often they had hardly any food, but the whole family shared whatever they had. A family of six or more would sit around an unsteady wooden table and eat a dinner of a few eggs, hard tortillas or bread and some potatoes, beans or corn. It made me wonder how the world's wealthy, the decision makers, or anyone in a position to help would feel if they could witness what I had during my time among the poor.

I had my own baby girl and wondered, could I ever stand seeing my child suffering the way these babies are? What would I do if I were facing the same circumstances as those indigent parents? I had always felt a great sympathy for the impoverished. I had been involved in assisting them since I was in high school in California, but when I saw Martha, a deep melancholy engulfed me because I was limited in what I could do. I had seen numerous poor children with big, happy smiles on their faces that had no idea what their parents endured in order to provide them with a home filled with love, with shelter, food, water, health care, and education. I made a promise to myself. I promised to do everything I could on behalf of the poor as long as I lived. But I also realized that in order to keep this promise, I had to impose upon myself stronger self–discipline, and more to the point, I needed to make money so I could help them. I was thirty-four years old. I made a decision to work harder and become better at management. I knew that with the right attitude and determination, I would eventually make my business grow, although it meant taking risks.

I myself had had insufficient money for medication or treatment after being injured when I worked as a police officer in Oxnard, California. Although it was not an extreme circumstance, I understood, however slightly, how poor mothers or fathers might feel if they did not have the means to provide for their families. The difference between my experience and their experiences was that mine was short-lived. Theirs were ongoing and could lead to crippling feelings of helplessness and despair. I told myself that I would not allow that to happen to anybody I had the power to help. I was growing. I now had another powerful, motivating purpose in my life. My family was my first priority. Moreover, I felt rewarded when I helped someone in need.

As the years passed, I became an investment and small business development advisor to European royalty. And I continued to assist the poor by teaching them how to manage or start up their own micro-businesses. My actions and my life purpose had come into alignment.

> *Whoever sows sparingly will also reap sparingly, and whoever sows*
> *bountifully will also reap bountifully. Each must do as already determined,*
> *without sadness or compulsion, for God loves a cheerful giver. God is able to*
> *make every grace abundant for you, so that in all things, always having all*
> *you need, you may have an abundance for every good work.*
>
> *2 Corinthians 6–8*

CHAPTER 2

Decisions in Life

———————

Some people seem to think that as long as they keep quiet, they have a sure chance of getting a fair treatment, but I have always felt that one must make a resolution to make changes and to succeed.

M y adventures as a child in Arizona were of the kind that many children have when they are eight, nine, or twelve. My experiences later in life were more diverse as I engaged life as a college student in California and later, after graduation, as a police officer; became a corporate employee, a global entrepreneur, an advisor, investor and international business professor; lived with the indigent in some exotic and interesting places in the world—India, Canada, Costa Rica, Ecuador, Peru, Guatemala, Spain, and Mexico. As a young boy, I met Robert Kennedy, and later in life, Rigoberta Menchú, the Guatemalan human rights activists who won the Nobel Peace Prize in 1992, Pope John Paul II, and the Dalai Lama. And I did research and consulting work so better strategic planning could be established for Latin America and the Caribbean area by World Vision, International, an excellent altruistic organization reaching out to the children of the poor.

As volunteer-teaching for ten years at San Jose Seminary with the Catholic Church in the Cuernavaca diocese, I taught seminarians how to apply economic strategies. These young men needed to be better managers of the offerings made to the church once they became ordained priests. I also became an advisor (and continue to be) to a wholeheartedly dedicated, much loved and highly respected diocese, Father Luis Millan.

While living in New York, I spent quality time with the homeless at Central Park in Manhattan on and off from 1998 until January 2011. That meant a lot to them as we spoke for hours, or shared a meal, whenever we met. It touched my heart to hear their stories of success and how they had become forgotten by their families. Some of these people had been wealthy business individuals or top executives at one time and had gone from riches to rags. In meeting these people, I always wondered how they got there. For many of them, drugs and alcohol were the cause of their downfall. How right the late Whitney Houston was when she indicated in her 2002 NBC interview "crack was wack." She also became a victim! Yes, drugs and alcohol had wacked many of the homeless I was meeting in Central Park. Drugs are not something to mess with. Drugs kill! And many more have lost their lives to drug or alcohol addiction.

People are singing and rapping about drugs these days, glamorizing drugs to younger generations who could end up dead too young, as too many of my friends have died.

Working With At-Risk Youth

The further I got involved, the more lessons I learned that motivated me to continue with this volunteer work. On February 2, 2011, my family and I, moved to Florida permanently, although we had lived here on a part-time basis since 1997. I became a mentor to young, at-risk boys at "Hands on Miami" until the program was cancelled in April due to a lack of funds. Not willing to accept this temporary set-back, in May I continued my volunteer services at an excellent program, the Empowered Youth Organization (EY), where boys aged thirteen to eighteen constantly soften my heart as I listened to their sad stories; stories a person does not want to believe. Some boys or girls were sexually abused by a relative, a sister's boyfriend, step-parents, and situations involving boyfriends or girlfriends of the parents.

They were teens who had committed an offense or at a very young age ran away from abusive foster homes in Alabama, Tennessee, Louisiana, or somewhere in Florida. We also had teens who arrived as children from Cuba, Honduras, El Salvador, Mexico, and the Dominican Republic. Some of these boys were forced to sell drugs as young six-year old children in order to have a meal on their table. And many other boys got involved in crime because they were influenced by no-good friends or could not get a job. On the other hand, many of the boys just had to be out on the streets because of the parents' drug and alcohol addiction, domestic violence, or other family dysfunction.

Being able to help these boys in any way gives me a feeling of worth, and most importantly, it benefits people who are not as fortunate. Although it may look incredible, many of these young boys are intelligent and are looking forward to an opportunity in life, and it is this attitude of perseverance that penetrated deep into my soul. However, being involved with these at-risk boys is an enormous responsibility, and at times I have become frustrated or upset. Other times, I have been threatened during the course of my duties.

While it is a worthwhile and much needed service, this type of volunteerism can be dangerous. For example, during one of our evening meetings at the EY center in Liberty City, two students—Santiago and John—were constantly arguing during class. As the argument escalated, it became very aggressive and almost resulted in a fight. I asked Santiago to walk out of the classroom with me. Carlos Valdes, the administrator, addressed the situation with John. As I was attempting to speak with Santiago, to my surprise, he suddenly produced a switchblade from his pants, placed the sharp blade on my throat, and said, *"This is how fast I can kill anyone here…but I respect you and love you… That bastard has been bothering me in class for several weeks and I am tired of him. I am going to hurt that boy one of these days."* I was afraid he would cut my throat, so maintaining my composure, I very calmly asked Santiago to remove the blade from my neck and we continued our dialogue.

At 16, Santiago had a strong physique—6 feet and 210 pounds—but was a shy and mellow youth. He hardly spoke in our meetings and was very attentive when addressed by staff. He had been involved in a couple of burglaries, and a judge had assigned him to our program instead of incarceration. He was being medically treated for schizophrenia.

I asked Santiago several times to give me his switchblade, to no avail. As we continued with our conversation, he finally removed the blade from my neck and started playing with the switchblade by flipping it open and closed with his right hand. He had his big, left arm around my shoulders, hugging me tightly and saying how much he appreciated me for attempting to help him since his arrival. After I pleaded with Santiago for the seventh or eighth time to give me his knife or to put it away in his jeans pocket, he finally did. I spoke firmly with Santiago during our dialogue, but I chose my words very carefully so as not to make a mistake and upset him. It took me about half an hour to calm him down. After we were done talking, I immediately told the Program Director that I was concerned that Santiago could hurt someone in the program. Carlos and I transported Santiago to his home. He never returned to our meetings.

I had encounters with two other boys who threatened me because I would not give them money or purchase a car for one of them. I stopped volunteering at EY in December 2012.

In July 2012, I became a volunteer teaching entrepreneurship and leadership courses at the Miami-Dade County Corrections & Rehabilitation Department's "I'm Ready" Boot Camp Program, invited by Collen Adams, the EY founder and executive director, and Judge Beth Bloom of the Eleventh Judicial Circuit of Florida. This program was set up to empower 14 to 23 year old incarcerated men and women by teaching them a skilled trade and learning proper behavior so they could become productive citizens in society, once released. I am very proud to say that since my involvement in the program, I have wholeheartedly participated with each student in the last six graduating classes. The graduates have embraced this opportunity given to them.

> *Whoever is dependent on his or her money or worries about it, is truly a*
> *poor person. If that person places his or her money at the service of others,*
> *then the person becomes rich, very rich indeed.*
>
> Mother Theresa

Not everything is rosy in life, nor am I a guardian angel; I have made mistakes I regret, like losing over two million dollars to "Bernie" Madoff'-type cronies. I was going to use the funds in special programs with the Catholic Church to help the poor in their university education. However, a lesson that I learned is that I became greedy. I wanted to make more money and did not withdraw when I had the chance. I learned about my demons. I have also erred and hurt people I love dearly. I have not kept all my promises.

I have felt extreme anger because I felt helpless. I have felt fear. Thoughts came to my mind in which I clearly saw my wife's and daughter's faces and said to myself, "My God, please help me. I am not going to see them again." Such a time occurred when I was "express kidnapped" in México City. After thirty or forty minutes in the kidnappers' hands, I knew that I was going to be killed. I prayed, became serene, and was ready to die. How curious it is, as one hears stories of what people feel when their last minutes of life arrive, that usually we do not think about those feelings or final thoughts. I will never forget that moment. I became frightened. I thought of a way to escape but it was too risky, as I still had hope that they would let me go. I wanted to cry; I was afraid. And then I had a calm sensation. I guess I automatically programmed by mind to die when I realized that I could not do anything.

I started to make conversation with the kidnapper who was guarding me in the taxi's back seat; I was pleading with him in a low voice to let me go, and explained that I was doing important work that helped the poor. I could see that the hard expression in his face changed; I noticed a sympathetic look. I told him to see the photos I had in my portfolio of the children I helped. He calmed down and became more humane as he was seeing each of the photos. He continued beating me, but his blows diminished considerably.

Education Is Essential

As a lifetime goal, I have attended several universities around the world because I had to be better qualified than my competitors as an entrepreneur, a consultant, an investor, and especially as a university professor. I wanted to be well prepared academically so I could share my knowledge and practical business know-how with my students. Becoming a sales manager at Johnson & Johnson; a strategic planning manager, and later a global entrepreneur gave me the opportunity to learn and corroborate organizational concepts I had learned in postgraduate work in college. There were some theories I did not agree with because they were not applicable in actual business situations. My undergraduate education at the University of California, Santa Barbara, gave me specific hands-on knowledge, the discipline to think, and helped me to become a better person. But I needed much more knowledge to prepare for business and life's challenges, which I later acquired with business experience as well as several degrees in graduate school.

Hard Times

Being a police officer taught me about the ugliness of some human beings, the wonders of many, and helped me become aware of what people are capable of doing under different circumstances—a surprise, indeed, when one is young and naïve.

I was a young man who had just graduated from the University of California. Filled with dreams and hopes, I was waiting for an opportunity. I had decided to become a police officer to help my community, especially teenagers. I did this in large part by persuading young people to stay away from drugs—the killer of the young, the affluent and those not so fortunate, of family unity, and of societies worldwide. I had been working continuously with students since I walked into the Oxnard Police Department in the summer of 1975. I visited my Alma Mater, Oxnard High School, late that summer; and different community centers thereafter to speak about drugs and their effects. I was also making plans to start law school in two or three years. But destiny had other plans, and my life took a distinctive twist after I was injured on the job. The injury occurred while on duty making a felony arrest during a rape in progress. I was hit multiple times on the head with my police flashlight. I survived, but was forced to take a completely different path in my life.

I spent months seeing physicians a psychiatrists and visiting hospitals where I was tested like a guinea pig. I had needles placed in my spine, in the veins in my arms, in my aorta, and everywhere else doctors could stick them, so they could find out why my dizzy spells, momentary unconsciousness, and extreme headaches continued. Most frighteningly, I completely passed out on several occasions. This happened once while I was driving home. I passed out and hit a parked post-office mail car. Another time I lost consciousness while on patrol and hit a railroad bridge. Brain scans were performed on me several times. The doctors were mystified by the symptoms. I thought, "What the hell do they expect after being clobbered on the head over ten times with a heavy police flashlight?" Doctors offered no solutions. What they did offer was a number of prescription medications aimed at reducing my pain. I took eight or nine of these prescribed pills every day, at five-to six-hour intervals. The side effects they created were almost worse than the symptoms, but at least they helped me, at times, with my pain. But these side effects were exhausting, and I felt as if I was floating all day.

To make matters worse, a lieutenant at the police station began constantly harassing me during my convalescence for being taken out of patrol and placed in an office job answering incoming calls. He would constantly ask me in a derogatory way, "Why are you taking all those pills?" Or "When are you going back out to patrol, Pinzón?" Many times he placed his face extremely close to mine and said in an intimidating manner, "Are you doing drugs again, Pinzón?" I responded to him that he knew very well that I had been injured on the job and that I was taking prescribed medication given to me by doctors and a psychiatrist; but he didn't care about my situation. He continued with his constant harassment for months.

One day, while I was in the dispatcher's room, this same lieutenant started harassing me about my pain as he had done on previous occasions. That day, however, I had reached my limit. I exploded. I told him that if he bothered me again, he and I were going to have it out and I was going to take a shot at him. He became very alarmed and hurried to the chief's office on the second floor. Within a few minutes, I received a phone call from my psychiatrist. He asked me what had happened. I told him about the incident with the lieutenant. He asked if I would really take a shot at him, and after pausing for a few seconds, I said no. I continued, "This man has been bothering me so much, over and over. I just exploded." My psychiatrist said that he wanted to see me in his office immediately that afternoon. He repeated himself three or four times, as though he wanted to make sure I would show up. I said, "Yes, I'll be there. I'll have my wife pick me up and take me to your office."

It was a breezy afternoon, and I could smell the sea. It was a cool, salty smell. The sun was three quarters in the zenith. I was staring at the mountain range north of us, which had some snow on the summit. My wife continued driving, speaking only to ask me a few questions. My responses were short and dry. I could see that she was offended by my attitude. I apologized, and she smiled. I was putting her through so much stress, which she did not need. Her father was a retired army captain in Mexico, so she was accustomed to a different lifestyle; but nonetheless, my attitude and the stress of the situation were taking their toll. I felt helpless, frustrated, disappointed, and discouraged. I felt miserable thinking of how my wife was putting up with my problems and me--the tribulations I was having with the city after my injury, my headaches, and my many sleepless nights. Her hair started to fall out from the stress. Life had been smiling at me five years earlier, and now my life was descending. I was sinking down a deep, dark tunnel and could not see the bottom. My whole world was being destroyed in front of me. "I was doing my duty as a police officer," I constantly told myself. "Why? What have I done?" I had no answers. And now I was surrounded by demons.

We continued southbound on Highway 101 toward Los Angeles when my wife pulled over to the side of the roadway. She stopped the vehicle and kissed me on the cheek. She embraced me and said, "I love you. I am your wife and will always be with you. Whatever decision you make, I am here with you. I'll continue teaching at Oxnard Junior College, and with that money, we'll do okay. Don't worry about anything." At that moment I realized the importance of having someone love me the way my wife did and having her next to me. She stayed with me through this period in my life; it was her love that kept me alive.

We finally arrived at my psychiatrist's home in Westlake where he had an office. He talked to me in his bedroom. He was in his robe. He spoke about the wonderful possibilities in life, about getting a new job, and he suggested that I take off for a while, maybe to Mexico to see my brother-in-law and his wife who, incidentally, were doctors. "You need to get away from this environment. Go take care of yourself and find something else to do." He advised me to leave the state because I was having too many problems, and he was worried that I might end up hurting the lieutenant who was harassing me at work.

Weeks later, I took his advice and voluntarily resigned from the force. During my resignation Chief Owens, my superior, told me, "I'm sorry, Miguel. I don't know what to do. I don't know how to grab this bull by the horns. I have attempted to do so, but my hands are tied. I wish you hadn't made matters worse by threatening the lieutenant." I responded, "Is it acceptable for a supervisor to continuously harass subordinates and for us not to say anything? What are we supposed to do? Just keep quiet? I filed a complaint against the lieutenant for his constant harassment, and he didn't stop."

When the conversation ended, I thanked the chief and walked out of his office, accompanied by the Oxnard Police Officer Association President, Officer Hurliman. I resigned as a police officer without receiving any benefits. A month passed and I called Chief Owens for a letter of recommendation. He said, "You know I will do anything for you. You can call me for anything that you may need." I picked up the letter from Chief Owens' office in May 1981 and thanked him. I walked away feeling worse than a leper who was not wanted by anyone; I felt betrayed by my own people. I understood the chief's political position. I had no idea what was going to happen with my life. I had little money. But worst of all, I felt betrayed by some of my fellow officers. The police department had been my life.

I did not want to ask for Social Security benefits, welfare stipends, or a handout from anybody. I wanted to work. I was young, strong, and smart. But I was still having awful headaches. I did not receive any medical benefits from the city after my resignation. My wife told me she agreed with my psychiatrist and believed it would be best to travel to Mexico and see if her brother could help me with my problems. Many times she told me, "We should try it."

I did not want to move to Mexico because I did not know anybody there. And truthfully, I was afraid to make the change. My mother and my two sisters lived close by in Ventura and Oxnard, and I was very happy in the town where I had lived since the sixth grade. I still had $5,000 from my police pension in my name and a condominium that I had purchased after graduating from college. I couldn't bring myself to leave everything I knew and loved.

Instead, I looked for a new job. Nobody wanted to hire me. I found, wherever I applied, I was blacklisted. After numerous interviews over a period of four months in the Los Angeles and Ventura County private sectors, a personnel manager who had interviewed me for a position in his company told me, echoing what my psychiatrist had said, "I'll be honest with you, Miguel. I've seen you twice, and I enjoyed our conversations. You seem to be a good man and an intelligent person. But nobody is going to hire you in California because when we called the city [my ex-employer], we got a negative response about you. I would suggest that you move out of the state and go to Arizona or Nevada. You should be able to find a job there." I thanked him for his honesty – finally, although not what I wanted to hear, I had a solid "reason" as to why I was unable to find work. I could not prove discrimination in court, and I did not want to fight the system. I was tired. I felt hurt and betrayed by the City of Oxnard's Risk Management Office manager. His private detectives lied or only told half-truths in the Workers' Compensation Court about my activities during my convalescence. There was a rumor at the police department that I wanted an early retirement and wanted to move to Mexico. When I heard these rumors, I thought, "And what am I going to do there?" It was ridiculous. In those years, many city officials around the area and in different police departments attempted to find an excuse or made up stories so they would not have to pay any benefits to injured police officers. Incidentally, I was declared thirty-three percent disabled by the State of California Workers' Compensation Judge.

During the six years that I had been a police officer, I had been a very responsible officer; I had cared for my community. I was a dependable employee who had received several letters of commendation from citizens about my commitment and rectitude toward my community and from my own chief of police.

In August of 1981--feeling frustrated and betrayed, in ill health, and out of work--my wife and I left our home in Port Hueneme, California, in the care of my sister, and I disappeared. The city lost a responsible police officer the easy way because I never wanted to file a lawsuit for benefits or retirement. My self-esteem, my world, and my life were shattered. I felt humiliated. I was heading to Mexico, uncertain about what I would find there, but certain that it could not be any worse than what I was leaving behind. And I threw away most of the pain pills I had been taking.

We drove for two days through long, isolated, hot desert roads. We met beautiful people in Tucson, Arizona, who told us what to do when crossing the U.S.-Mexican border in El Paso, Texas. Their tips gave me courage when we crossed the border into Juarez at 11:30 p.m. a day later. My vehicle and small trailer were thoroughly inspected by two Mexican Immigration officers, and I was asked numerous questions. I was also asked to give a bribe and refused to give the officers any money. One of them wanted to confiscate property, and I indicated that if he took anything, I was going to file a complaint. I did not have any contraband; nevertheless, he wanted a small oil painting we had. I became very nervous and thought of giving up this crazy idea of moving to Mexico. About an hour or so later, the officers approved our entrance into the country, and numerous seals were placed on the trailer.

We drove away from the border town of Juarez, and a couple of hours later my wife and I attempted to sleep in the car, parked in an isolated area off the highway. The night was pitch dark as my wife and I exchanged several thoughts about the trip and our future; and as I continued speaking, she fell asleep. The sky was beautiful, filled with thousands of bright stars. The sight fascinated me. I kept on wondering if I had made the right decision. As I contemplated the stars, the cool breeze flowed through my opened window and caressed my face. I had no other alternatives, I thought. I fell asleep and woke up close to 6 a.m. We continued on our way, driving deeper south into the country. Finally, two days later, we drove into Cuernavaca, Morelos, where my wife's family was waiting for us. Her parents, a sister, five brothers and their children greeted us when we arrived. We lived with my in-laws for almost three years.

A few days after our arrival, my brother-in-law took me to see several of his doctor friends who performed tests on me and prescribed different injections to ease my pain whenever I needed it. I did not feel any improvement. I felt useless, as if life was slipping away from my hands. I had many negative thoughts, including thoughts of giving up on life. I joined a Krishna group, searching for new concepts in my existence. One particular morning, I realized how strong my wife's love was towards me, and how her family cared for my well-being. I had known the family since I was a small child. How could I have been vacillating with such a self-pity and destructive thoughts? I changed my attitude and stopped feeling sorry for myself. What happened to me, I thought, happens to many people; that's part of life. I had to face reality and start doing something to place my life in the proper order. I had decided that I was going to learn to live with my health problems. I became involved with the Catholic Church and after having several conversations with Cuernavaca's human rights activist, Bishop Sergio Mendez Arceo, I realized just how fortunate I was to be alive. And more importantly, I met many people who cared for me. I decided to start a new life, in a different profession.

I ended up in a completely different field of work. Life is full of surprises! Seven months after my resignation from law enforcement, I finally found work, first as sales manager for Johnson & Johnson, and later as a strategic planning and logistics manager in a manufacturing company. I became an entrepreneur in

1986, and in 1992 I was hired as an adjunct professor. In 1995, I started writing about business ethics, international business, entrepreneurship, economics, and management. I have taught entrepreneurship for over twenty years in several countries, in Latin American campuses, and in the MBA and undergraduate programs at the prestigious Tec de Monterrey (ITESM), a technological and business school. This university promotes faculty and student exchanges with over 80 famous institutions throughout the world developing academic and research projects. I also taught in the undergraduate and MBA programs in the Executive MBA Florida International University, Florida National University, the University of the Americas, and other universities.

When I became a professor, I was determined to teach my practical business experiences to young entrepreneurs. My goal was to guide them, so they would not make the same mistakes I made when I started in business.

Practice proves more than theory.
A. Lincoln

CHAPTER 3

La Historia de Mi Familia

———— ❦ ————

MY FAMILY'S STORY

Never make fun of people who speak broken English;
it means they speak more than one language.

Author Unknown

I am very proud to say that I was born in Colima, one of the smallest states in Mexico, which is also its capital. When I remember Colima, what comes to mind are the coconut palm trees, the lemon and mango orchards growing in endless rows, and the warm and friendly people. I also remember the sun that follows you along the cobblestone streets, or on the warm water at the beach in Tecomán, a town approximately forty miles south of the state's capital. And to complete the picture, the breathtaking scenery of the volcano of fire, as it is called by everyone, or *El Volcan de Colima*, which is currently one of the most active volcanoes in the country and in North America. It has erupted over sixty times since 1576 and has been constantly smoking since I could remember as a child. Despite its name, a small fraction of the volcano's surface area is in the state of Colima; the majority of the volcano lies in the neighboring state of Jalisco. A second dormant volcano can also been seen from different places in the city, the *Nevado de Colima.* The movie *10* with Bo Derek was filmed at beautiful *Las Hadas* hotel in the port of Manzanillo, Colima.

I lived in the state of Sonora for seven years of my childhood prior to immigrating to the United States in June of 1963. My father, Salvador, a golden gloves boxer in Colima when he was seventeen years old, was a tailor; and my mother, Maria Guadalupe, was a seamstress. Everyone who knew her called her *Lupe.* They moved to Caborca, Sonora, in 1955 when I was three years old and opened a small business. Caborca was a small town with three thousand inhabitants, a church with two high towers, and two kiosks. While living there, I attended an elementary Catholic school, and the nuns treated me with much love and discipline; especially my teacher, Sister Lily, whom I still call every Christmas season.

I remember seeing my father working every day from 7:00 a.m. to 9:00 p.m. six days a week. He was a tailor. My mother had special customers who brought their long, elegant, silk dresses and exclusive gabardines, made from expensive Italian and English fabrics, for cleaning and alteration. She washed them by hand using white gasoline, the best cleaning method at the time. She worked all week under the hot sun. The work was good, if seasonal.

My father had a second job. He represented a famous Mexican beer company and would cross the street to a casino every night after closing the business to promote *Tecate* beer. Every Friday and Saturday night, he stayed drinking beer with customers and friends until the sun rose on the horizon, fat and orange in the morning sky. "Contact marketing," he called it. It was a marketing concept he conveniently learned quickly to promote the product, and the job would severely affect his health in later years. My mother hated this job. She was right to hate it.

In the early 1970s, my father's drinking led to a series of hospitalizations. He was afflicted with acute cirrhosis of the liver. If people could only learn in time and become conscious of the serious effects heavy beer drinking can have.

My *papá* and *mamá*, as I called them, used to fight. She could envision the problem and insisted that his drinking would ruin his life and the lives of his family. They never divorced, though, as much as they threatened it, maybe because we practiced Catholicism and we were closely attached to our traditions. And more to her roots, a chauvinistic society prevailed. Instead, in June 1963 my whole family emigrated to the United States. During those years the immigration process was different. Yes, all the documentation had to be submitted, and we had a series of interviews in Nogales, Arizona. Coming to the United States was a learning process. We had to adapt to a new culture and learn the language and traditions. But we were all very happy, as my mother had emigrated several months before we did, living and working at *La Posta Quemada* Ranch in Vail, Arizona, and I had not seen her during that time. The family was going to be together once more.

My father worked in different jobs during our first year in Arizona. He worked in a restaurant washing dishes, later as a cowboy and mechanic with the owners of the ranch where we lived, and repaired highway patrolmen's uniforms in a couple of tailoring shops in Tucson.

My mother was a disciplinarian. She was a hardworking woman who drove the family to work hard and save money because she wanted us to have a home. She also understood the importance of knowing English and registered in night school the following year when we moved to California so she could learn it. I accompanied her three nights a week until I was a sophomore in high school. As a boy, I lived to make her proud; but it was difficult to please her due to her authoritarian character.

In July 1964, we moved to California. My mother attended beauty school after work and later worked as a part-time beautician. She also worked in a lemon and celery packing house. In her mind was a dream home, and she would not rest until it became a reality. Both of my parents worked two or three jobs at the same time for several years. It took four years until they finally had enough money for a deposit to purchase our home. My mother worked throughout her life, although she had saved a good amount of money for retirement. She continued working in one of her businesses, a care home for former drug addicts, until she was forced to stop due to a severe illness. She passed on at the age of seventy-three in November 2008 after a long struggle with diabetes.

Some of my stories in this book have a common denominator with many Mexican or other families who emigrated to the United States. My mother had a proud but somewhat tragic history, filled with people I would meet briefly, if ever. My maternal grandfather Miguel was one of them. He was always an obscure person to me. He gave away his eight-year-old girl, my mother, to her godmother. So it passed that my mother was raised in Colima, without her mother or father, by a lady whom I would only meet twice briefly. My mother kept in close contact with her guardian throughout her life and sent her money from California until she passed away, but she never allowed me to get close to her.

I met my mother's fifth-grade teacher in 1998, when I accompanied her to Pihuámo, Jalisco, and a town that is an hour's drive west of Guadalajara. My mother actually did not know if her teacher was still alive. I was impressed by how my mother was eagerly searching for her elementary school teacher. She had not seen her in decades. This person, I thought, must have made a strong impact on my mother, and I was looking forward to meeting her also. We drove into the small, colorful town in the early afternoon. "It has changed a lot," was the first thing my mother said about it. Every house I could see was painted in white and had reddish roof tiles; some were new, and many were covered with mold. It was picturesque. I could see the cobblestone streets were clean in every direction. I felt, wonderfully, as though I had stumbled back in time.

Pihuámo had a charming vitality. Men, women, and children had their wares set up on the sidewalk. They sold various types of freshly made Mexican sweet bread, tortillas, tacos, live chickens, pigs, different types of parrots, canaries, guacamayas, herbs, fruits, vegetables, pottery in diverse shapes and forms, and pans in many colors. The town was located on the skirt of a hill and was surrounded by a mountain range covered with trees and plants in distinctive greens, browns, and yellows. It was the rainy season when we visited. Thick cumulus clouds, painted gray and white and pierced here and there by the sharp rays of the afternoon sun, floated in the clean air above us. It looked as though it might begin to rain at any moment. When I inhaled, my nostrils were filled with the smell of fresh, wet earth. I was glad that I had taken my mother to her birth town and more so because she was searching for her roots. It appeared that she wanted to find out something missing about her childhood, her family, but she never spoke to me about it.

I felt happy for my mother when I observed the attentive expression on her face. She seemed pleased, and I noticed a few tears coming from her eyes. She tried to hide them from me. She was smiling. My mother soon recognized her school, a block away from the church with its double high towers, and she asked me to stop. She found her elementary teacher's home. It was made of adobe and brick. The teacher's family had lived there for over two centuries, and again I felt that curious sensation of the past commingling with present. I realized that learning about our own family roots is essential to everyone.

After the teacher's sister, whom my mother had not met before, invited us into the house, we waited for a time in a pink-colored living room. When the teacher finally entered, they recognized each other immediately despite the many years that had passed. We stood up to greet her teacher, and my mother and her dear old teacher hugged affectionately for a while. Her teacher, a lady in her mid-seventies said, "*Mi pequeña niña, no has cambiado nada, solamente crecido*" (my little girl, you have not changed at all—only grown).

We had lunch with her and drank freshly made guava juice as they spoke about their lives. They had not seen each other since the 1930s. They never spoke about my mother's family, although her teacher knew about them. When she mentioned them, my mother quickly changed the subject. I learned that my mother had been a very studious little girl and that she was always doing business in school. My mother never spoke about her childhood or her family when I was growing up, but I had seen her school report card. She had mostly As.

It was a very gratifying experienced learning that side of my mother's life. We should take the opportunity to get to know our real parents and know about their feelings, about their lives. Their upbringing molded our character and helped us become what we are. We must attempt to comprehend why they have certain attitudes we do not understand so we can become closer instead of growing further apart. Sometimes we forget about them, and later in life we learn how much we missed their love for us. What we must be certain of is that they will always love us. Parents are sacred.

Late afternoon had set in by the time we left. The heat and humidity were partially soothed by a light, cool breeze that caressed my face as I looked at the mountains above the old tile roofs visible downhill. As we walked, passing strangers greeted us with pleasant smiles. We walked about three blocks, stopping and my mother knocked on a wooden door. A young girl, barely a teenager, with a black, waist-length ponytail, answered, after my mother asked her a question, the young girl pointed to a home across the street and stated in Spanish, "*Ahí viven*" *(they live there)*. That was a quick response, I thought, as I remembered how I knew almost everyone in the small town in Sonora years back. They definitely knew me.

I knocked three times on an old but recently varnished door made of light brown wood. A lady with white hair answered. My mother recognized her immediately and greeted her. "*Hola tía, como está? El es mi hijo.*" (Hello, aunt, how are you? He is my son.) Her aunt looked surprised. She fixed her long, sandy hair and removed her apron. "*Pasa mi hija, como estás? Tiene más de cuarenta años que no se de ti?*" (Come in, my daughter. How are you? It has been over forty years since I heard anything about you).

We walked into the house, and the lady spoke a bit about my mother's family. We learned that all of my mom's brothers and sisters had been living in different places in United States since the late 1950s. My mother appeared a little annoyed and told her that she did not want to hear anything about her father; she only wanted to know about her mother, Heliodora. Our visit there lasted about forty-five minutes. As they spoke, I looked at several 1800s photographs hanging on the living room wall. I also noticed the pleasant smell of fresh bread coming from the back of the house. I could see a young lady, a distant cousin I was meeting for the first time, in the back of the house baking Mexican bread.

It started to rain for a few minutes, and the middle patio of the house, filled with flowers and birds in their cages, which had been singing since our arrival, filled the house with life. A few minutes later, the rain stopped. The smell of wet earth was stronger than before. The smell reminded me of when I was a small child and visited my grandmother in Colima, about forty miles southwest of my mother's town. A large river that had a rapid current during the rainy season, the jungle, a couple of villages, and three volcanoes separated the two towns.

My mother's aunt walked into an adjacent room and brought back an old wooden box filled with black-and-white photographs. That afternoon I learned that my mother was the youngest of seventeen children, and she was about seven years younger than her older sister. Her aunt also showed us an 8" x 6" faded black-and-white photo of my mother's family. Mother pointed to a little girl and said, "*Soy yo*" (that's me). She named all of her brothers and sisters as she pointed at each of them. She then held her hand in the middle of the photo, pointing at a middle-aged lady with black hair, rested her finger, and in a low voice, as though speaking to herself said, "My mother." I noticed tears standing in her eyes, but she composed herself quickly. I held her hand softly, and she smiled.

Her aunt, standing next to us, pointed to herself in the photo and said, "*Soy yo. Tenía veinticinco*" (That's me. I was twenty-five). I noticed that almost everyone in the photo had light-colored hair. I had never heard much about my grandmother—again I think about that silence my mother possessed concerning these matters' and I had not seen a photo of her family before.

Nevertheless there were a few things my mother shared about her family when I was growing up. When I was about fourteen, my mother told me that her father was a handsome but mean man, with dark blue eyes, black hair, and thick eyebrows. He took his whole family to live on an isolated ranch in the mountains several miles outside Pihuámo. This was one of the only things she ever volunteered about her family.

There was something else as well. The truth was that I had known the origin of my mother's lifelong grief for some time, and being in Pihuámo with her aunt placed it all the more firmly in my mind. When I was eighteen, I wanted to visit my mother's hometown to see my grandmother and search for her family. My mother forbade it. I demanded to know why and I received a terrible, unexpected answer. "I was given away because of my fair skin and black hair." She remembered her brothers and sisters all having blond hair and green or blue eyes. She asked me not to look for those people, the ones who gave her away. "They have been dead to me ever since I was a little girl." I canceled my trip. We never spoke of it again.

My paternal family was the complete opposite of my mother's. My father's family was always around when we visited my *abuelitos* (grandparents) in Colima when I was a child. My father had five brothers and three sisters. I remember there were always children and cousins running around my abuelitos' home when I visited them. My uncles and aunts lived near my grandmother until her death in 1987.

My grandfather, Celedonio, was a tall, lean, proud man. He had fought in the Mexican Revolution (1910-1920), joining Pancho Villa's forces against the federal government when he was thirteen or fourteen years old. He was never shy about why he had joined the revolution. *"Los ricos cometieron muchas injusticias contra los pobres, y el gobierno lo permitia"* (The wealthy committed many injustices toward the poor, and the government permitted it), he said. The Mexican Revolution represented to its people a promise of a better life and social justice for all. Today this has still not come to pass, and many changes must occur to reach those dreams.

My grandfather became a successful small business entrepreneur after the revolution. My uncle, his older brother, was a tall, husky, and modest man, with a big white moustache, whom I admired for his knowledge of world history. He was a captain in the federal forces during the revolution and fought against my grandfather's "insurgency contingent," as he called it. This revolution separated families; brothers fought against brothers. The same characteristic occurred in the US Civil War (1861–1865), the French Revolution (1789–1799), and the Russian Revolution (1917), when these countries became divided and brothers fought brothers in the name of social justice. People fought to defend the oppressed.

During the years I visited my grandfather and his brother, they would argue as to which side had been right during the Mexican Revolution. They kept their distance and seldom spoke to each other for over sixty years, although they lived only thirty yards apart. During my visits to Colima, I attempted to reconcile them, but to no avail. However, when my grandfather did not recollect an event about the revolution, he would tell me, "*Ve pregúntale a tu tío, quiza el recuerde*" (Go ask your uncle; he might remember), and vice versa. I last saw them in July 1973, at my father's funeral services. After the funeral they finally made their peace. However, they had lost valuable time due to their pride, as they could have lived a wonderful life as family but instead never got to know each other well. My grandfather died the year after my father's passing, and the federal government's Twentieth Army Battalion in the state capital of Colima sent an official ceremonial honor guard to pay their respects to my grandmother; and to my grandfather for his service during the revolution.

My paternal grandmother went by the nickname "*Chenchita.*" The "*ita*" when added to a name makes it diminutive and is used when a person is deeply loved or appreciated, and she most assuredly was. Her given name was Crecencia. She was a peaceful and well-educated woman, six or eight years older than my grandfather. When I visited her as a small child during the summer, she made sure to spoil me with many delights of Mexican culinary traditions, taking me to a different world of delicious tastes and flavors and making me feel very much loved. She would make my favorite drink for breakfast every day—hot, rich, Mexican chocolate. She would often take me to the street market, two blocks away from her home, at 6:00 a.m. There she would buy me sweet pumpkin and a glass of fresh raw milk. She convinced me that this milk was healthy for me. I had no idea if she was telling me the truth or not, but to me what mattered was that if she said it, that was the truth. She passed away in 1988 at the age of ninety-four.

Following a tradition of many Latin American families, my grandmother took care of her younger sister and my great-grandmother, Paula, who had a very strong character and was of pure Aztec descent. Paula was forever ordering everyone around. I remember her saying until the day she died, "No one will order me around, including the president. I have my own free will and will do as I please." Her husband, my great-grandfather Pedro, was a farmer. All of my ancestors from my grandmother's side of the family had lived in Colima since before the Spanish conquest of Mexico.

During a short visit to my grandmother's home when I was fourteen, I remember her showing me an old dagger that had belonged to my great-grandfather's family and was given to her by her father-in-law when she married my grandfather in the early 1920s. The dagger was about six or eight inches long and had a fancy gold handle engraved with different designs and a big white pearl and two small emeralds on each side of the handle. A faded inscription adorned the dagger's golden sheath: *"Para Los hermanos Pinzón por su valor...Isabel la Catolica. Reina de España. 1493"* (To the Pinzón brothers for their courage... Isabel the Catholic, Queen of Spain. 1493). My grandmother told me that she wanted me to have that dagger once I graduated from college, but after my father's death in 1973, many things disappeared from her home, including this relic. My only hope is that whoever kept this important item knows how to appreciate the cultural value it has and donates it to a museum.

Growing Up In Arizona

As I mentioned earlier, I grew up in Sonora, the border state south of Arizona, from the ages of three to eleven. After arriving in the United States in 1963, my family lived at *La Posta Quemada* Ranch in Vail, Arizona, for a year. This was a year of change for my family. We moved to a new country and began to learn about the culture; we exchanged a small town of three thousand inhabitants where I knew almost everyone for an isolated ranch of six people.

We were living at *La Posta Quemada* thanks to the generosity of Mr. Orel Burris, the owner of the ranch. He was a tall, strong, Texas cattle rancher who had helped us emigrate to the United States because he believed that my parents were hard workers and he wanted us to have a better life. He had been one of the customers at my parents' business in Sonora, where he had many American friends who were cattle ranchers.

Susanita, his wife, was a beautiful, tall, slim woman with a light brown complexion and dark brown eyes. She was part Cherokee. And treated us like her own family. She invited us to have our first Thanksgiving dinner in her home, along with three cowboys and their families who worked at the ranch. My mother worked for Susanita as a cook and acted as companion for her because Mr. Burris was constantly traveling, and she did not want to be alone. I also worked for Susanita when we arrived at *La Posta Quemada* Ranch. I had a job picking up nails on the ranch's dirt road where she drove, which was about a quarter mile long. I cleaned up the road during that summer, and she paid me a penny for every nail I turned in to her.

We were spending a few days with Susanita in the ranch's big house when President John Kennedy was assassinated on November 22, 1963. Susanita cried throughout the days leading up to the burial, and she explained to me in detail what was going on and what the assassination meant to the country. She spoke to me about American history and the importance of liberty and justice and how the political process worked, and she insisted that I must go to college and help people in need. As she caressed my head, she also mentioned that it was time for me to start being a young man. Later in life I understood the charismatic personality JFK had and the greatness he represented to the United States.

Five months after our arrival in November, I started working weekends at the Colossal Cave and received five dollars a day for working five hours. I was almost twelve and without being conscious of my tender age, I was initiating my working career. Susanita helped me get the job. She spoke with the manager of the Cave, Mr. Joe Maierhauser and his lovely wife Martie; they hired me. My duties were to keep the grounds clean and place cardboard signs that read "Visit Colossal Cave, Vail Arizona," on the cars of tourists visiting the cave. I usually placed forty signs, but on especially busy days I would place sixty or more.

When I ran out of signs, the guides would take me into the cave with the tourists. An Apache medicine man whose family had lived in the area since ever told me that his ancestors had used the cave to cure people afflicted by evil spirits and for other ceremonies. The cave's stalactite and stalagmite formations dated back thousands of years, and even today is still an important tourist attraction beside the Saguaro National Park nearby and Old Tucson, twenty-two miles away. Many changes have occurred at the Colossal Cave since I left in 1964. It has now become a very important tourist attraction, and *La Posta Quemada* ranch has become part of the Colossal Cave Mountain Park. Joe passed away in 2007 after managing the cave since 1956, and lovely Martie continues at the park.

Sometimes on Saturdays when he did not work and on Sundays after Mass, my father would take me to work in his white-and-light-blue '56 Chevy coupe, but I usually walked. Colossal Cave, which was up on a mountain, could be seen from my home at the ranch, and I enjoyed my mile walk from *La Posta Quemada* to work. As I walked up and down the hills leading to the cave, I searched diligently for arrowheads. After working for about three months, I was trained by a young Apache guide to be his aide. I felt very important. I recall fondly that tourists loved to hear me when I explained in my broken English about certain places in the cave. Here is where I began to learn the importance of human relations and the essence of giving an excellent service, as it showed in the tips I received from the tourists.

My favorite tale concerned three bandits who had hidden there after robbing a train near Tucson back in the late 1800s. The sheriff and his posse tracked them to the cave and waited outside for them to come out. They never did. Three days had passed when Virgil Earp (brother of famous Wyatt Earp), a lawman for Pima County who was then residing in Tombstone, arrived at the cave on his way to Tucson. He had heard about the bandit hunt and told the sheriff that the outlaws had been seen in Tombstone a couple of days earlier. The sheriff never found out how the bandits got out of the cave. To this very day, the secret exit has not been located.

I was very appreciative to my friend as I enjoyed the many stories or legends he would tell me in the solitude of living on a ranch without any other boys around. I spent many a day fantasizing about the history that had taken place there. There are other fascinating legends about the Colossal Cave that are based on fact, but in order to hear about them, visit the cave, and you decide for yourself which stories you believe.

My Apache friend had a partially disabled left arm. He told me that his arm had been pulled out of its elbow socket when he was a teenager. The incident occurred while he was lassoing a bull during a rodeo. He worked as a seasonal cowboy at the *La Posta Quemada* ranch when extra help was needed to round up or brand cattle. Jimmy Leon, Eddie, the Figueroa brothers, and other cowboys also worked there. Chico Lopez and Jimmy taught me how to ride a horse and lasso calves. I also helped do errands around the ranch, like bringing in firewood or helping feed the horses. It was awesome to be around the cowboys sharing their experiences.

My family and I had a wonderful time there. My year at the ranch holds some of the happiest memories of my life. A small lake, which was about one hundred yards from my home, offered a great deal of amusement to me. I attempted numerous times to fish there, but alas, my destiny was not to be a fisherman even though Mr. Burris, and his friends attempted to teach me. Early one evening I grabbed a fishing pole and tried my luck by myself. I waited while the sunlight died, bored and disappointed, when suddenly I saw a catfish swimming near the lake's edge. I could not find a worm to use as bait. I cursed my ill luck and wondered what I could do. I stood motionless until the fish reached the edge of the lake. I kneeled down, and to my surprise I caught the fish with my bare hands. I was overjoyed to have the catfish in my hand, but when I noticed that it was attempting to escape from my grasp, I felt sorry for the small creature. I threw it back into the water. I had beef jerky with beans for dinner that evening instead of a fish filet. Fishing and I were not meant to be; it requires a special skill and patience — and I did not have either.

I spent most of those warm summer days in '63 with the cowboys, but a large amount of the time, I was alone. I continued my search for arrowheads in the mountains and spent a great deal of time looking for Geronimo's gold. I found treasure hunting more interesting than fishing. My Apache friend's father had gotten me very enthusiastic about Geronimo's treasure by telling me a thrilling tale about it. Unfortunately, I was never able to find that legendary treasure during all my excursions, but I did have a great time in those days.

I remember a hot summer night in July or August. The sky was filled with stars, and a bright, silvery, full moon appeared in the firmament. It seemed close enough to touch with your bare hands. The night was pleasant and cool, a wonderful relief after the harshness of the day. I was sitting around a fire about one hundred yards outside my home, on top of a small hill, with several cowboys who were telling stories, drinking coffee, and eating pieces of beef jerky. To this day, my passion for beef jerky continues as I purchase it by pounds whenever I can. I carry it in my briefcase or in my jeans pocket so I can have a piece, as the urge for beef jerky is always with me.

There were the Figueroa brothers and Jimmy Leon, experienced cowboys whom Mr. Burris had hired that hot afternoon. In the evening, Jimmy told me that they were going to bring cattle to the ranch. I liked Jimmy; whenever I saw him, he never failed to give me a hunk of the sweet, delicious beef jerky he carried with him everywhere. Jimmy asked me if I wanted to go with them to bring in the cattle the following morning at 6:00 a.m. and said to meet them at the ranch's corral. I responded, "Okay, I want to go. But I have to ask my mother." He then told me to go home and get some rest because we were going to have a long day.

I ran home and told my parents about the invitation. My mother gave me permission to go. I could not sleep that night. I was excited and restless about accompanying the cowboys the following morning. I felt the world of adults opening to me and felt privileged to be included in it. I kept staring at the full moon lighting up the mountains through my window. I could clearly see the moon's light reflecting on the lake's surface. The sky was filled with stars. I let my imagination go wild that evening as I tossed in my bed from one side to another. I got up and continued staring at the moon and the mountains from my window.

The ranch was in a small valley and was surrounded tightly by mountains. I could see that all the lights were out in the other two homes in the ranch. The Burris lived in the big house, and they rented a medium-sized house to a banker who lived there with his wife and their baby. We lived in the small house. My imagination continued to run wild. I was thinking about how I would lasso an untamed horse and bring it in peacefully to the ranch's corral, already broken by my youthful prowess. More thoughts came. I fantasized about becoming a cowboy later in life and having my own cattle ranch. I thought about finding Geronimo's gold. I probably fell asleep at around 2:00 a.m.--and did not wake until up around 7:00 a.m. That morning, my mother found a note written in pencil posted on the front door. She gave it to me. It said, simply, "See you later in the afternoon at the corral." I had been left behind. My mother gave me a glass of raw milk, two eggs, and bacon for breakfast. Both my parents left for work soon thereafter. I grabbed my cowboy hat and ran to the corral about a quarter mile from my home, but I did not find anybody there. My cowboy dreams were dashed for the moment.

It was a beautiful, warm summer morning. The sun was coming out from behind the big mountain east of me, and I could feel that it was going to be another hot day. I waited until I saw Mr. Burris's horse and a pony that belonged to his twelve-year-old daughter Cindy. I had met her twice. She did not live at *La Posta Quemada*. I retrieved Mr. Burris' horse, a big animal with a reddish-brown coat and a white star formation on its forehead. I took a rope from the small barn and lassoed the horse's neck, but I could not get him to lie down. After several attempts, I walked him over to the corral's fence. I climbed up and jumped on the horse's back. As the horse felt my body on his back, it ran toward the opposite side of the corral. I held on tightly with my legs and grabbed its mane with both hands. The horse ran faster and faster and stopped suddenly --and I was airborne, flying right over the corral fence. I stayed on the ground where I had landed and noticed a cloud of dust over me. My Levis was torn on both knees. I saw blood running down my legs. I stared back at the horse. As the first few tears were forming in my eyes, I sat there for a few minutes, blowing on my knees and attempting to remove the dirt and blood from my scraped knees. It stung miserably. I finally stood up, dusted myself off, and resolved to find the cowboys who were on the other side of the mountain. I removed the rope from the horse and started walking to find the cowboys. They were two or three miles away, about an hour's walk from the corral.

The sun got hotter as morning gave way to noon. To escape from the worst of the heat, I decided to walk along the dry, sandy river. I made my way in the shade under a eucalyptus tree to a marked path that led to the mountaintop. I was playing, throwing rocks at the rabbits I saw in my path. After I got bored with this, I began picking up the strangest stones I could find. I pretended that I had finally found Geronimo's elusive gold.

While scrutinizing an especially promising stone, I noticed that a coyote was walking downhill on the same path, and we were going to meet. I was stunned. The coyote was about seventy or eighty yards away and getting closer. I stopped walking and started looking for a place where I could hide. "I have to get up a tree," I thought. My survival instincts came to mind rapidly. Looking right, I could see only some dried-out cacti and many tall saguaros along the mountainside. The dry, barren mountain continued as far as I could see. There was no place to hide. The dry, sandy river was on my left. The coyote was getting closer.

Something important I had learned about survival from my Apache cowboy friend was to never show that I was frightened of anything. "We must always be proud of ourselves and have dignity," he used to tell me. "Regardless of the situation you find yourself in, if a horse smells that you're afraid, you will never be a good cowboy. Be courageous." His advice was wise, and it became important to me for later life events. I liked him very much. His words resonated with something my father used to say. He often told me, "If something happens to me, you will take care of your mother and sisters. That will always be your responsibility."

I had been forced to grow up quickly. The chores I had to perform at home kept me out of mischief. I had to take care of my sisters, wash the dishes after breakfast, sweep the patio, and feed the chickens and pigeons we owned. After the housework was finished, my mother had me study my multiplication tables for two hours. Suddenly, all that homework didn't seem to matter. Multiplication was no good against coyotes. Still, I wasn't completely helpless. I decided to do what I had learned from my dear Apache friend. "I must have the same courageous attitude toward this coyote," I thought. Brave words, but I was still scared. I had a knife with a four-inch blade, which my Apache friend had given me. I took it out of its sheath that hung on my belt. My knees trembled. I looked over to my left; it was very steep. The river bottom was about fifteen yards down and held nothing but sand. I did not dare to jump. I watched the coyote come closer. I noticed its open mouth, saliva dripping. His tongue hung loosely between sharp teeth. The coyote stopped unexpectedly and stared at me. At that exact moment I ran down the hill as fast as I could. I looked back and noticed that the coyote was no longer advancing, but I continued running.

I saw a small tree filled with branches on the riverside. Without thinking, I threw myself on the branches and attempted to hold onto them as I was falling down the tree. I tumbled against the tree, my hands clutching in desperation. They finally found a branch and I hung on. I pulled myself against the tree, my chest heaving. As the shock faded, I began to notice that both of my sides hurt. I could barely catch my breath. I felt a few sharp scratches on my face. I stayed in the tree for almost an hour until I was sure that the animal was gone. I climbed down the tree, walked over to a small stream in the river, and went swimming. I decided not to look for my cowboy friends, as I did not want to encounter that coyote again.

I had been playing in a pool of water for about an hour when I heard a cowboy yelling my name, "Michael! Michael!" as a couple of the cowboys used to call me. His voice was booming. I yelled back and saw Chico Lopez galloping toward me on his horse. He had found my cowboy hat on the riverbed and gotten worried that something had happened to me. This was not the first time I had gone into the mountain looking for them, and he knew how intrepid I was. He figured that I was playing in the area, but what seemed strange to him was that I had left my hat behind. Everyone at the ranch knew that I loved my cowboy hat. I had seen the hat on the TV Show *Maverick*, and a cowboy friend I mentioned it to had purchased it for me in Old Tucson.

I would never leave my cowboy hat anywhere unless there was a dire emergency. Before the coyote incident, I had lost my hat only once. Bees had chased me when I attempted to get a piece of honeycomb from their hive, which I had discovered in the back of an abandoned storage room near the corral. There were several logs in the storage room. They were leaning against the back wooden wall, and there it was: a beehive filled with honey. Thoughtlessly I cut a piece from the hive with my knife, and dozens of bees were immediately after me. I ran for about fifty or sixty yards. During my long run, I was stung several times on my neck and face. When I finally returned home, I slept the entire day. One of the cowboys found my hat the following day. It was being blown by the wind on the prairie where I had dropped it while running from the bees.

Regardless of the dangers it held for an inquisitive child, I still remember *La Posta Quemada* Ranch as a beautiful place. It was an adventurous child's dream. I could never stand to stay home and be idle, although I did make time for a few television series like *Maverick*, *Bat Masterson*, *Gunsmoke*, *Superman*, and a new show that I loved when it came out in '64, *Destry*, my favorite TV series. *Destry* was my hero. I had the hat to prove it.

I'm sure in some way those shows ignited my enthusiasm for treasure hunting. Once, my Apache friend took several of my friends and me on an expedition to look for Geronimo's gold. To our surprise, my best friend from school, Willy, found an old, rusted Colt pistol. We went home with our finding. I told my two younger sisters about my treasure hunt, and they ignored me and continued playing with their dolls. My sisters were in their own world, and I was in mine. My father and mother never said anything about my treasure hunting; they would just tell me to be careful and not to come home late. At times I was suspicious that my Apache friends were making up stories so I would keep busy looking for the treasure and they could work in peace. They took care of me when I was with them. Sometimes I was an obstacle because they had to wait for me, but they were always friendly and patient; they took their time to teach me many things. Most importantly, these grown men kept my dreams going with their many stories, and they all instilled in me the drive to do well in school and get a university education.

Legends Of Geronimo's Gold

This legend had a great effect on me, as I was constantly searching for that treasure while living at *La Posta Quemada*. There was another legend—that if you were in a certain place on the summit of the mountain on the west side of the valley—the treasure would reveal its location. As the sun rose, you had to look for the first ray of sun. It would strike a big rock, and that ray would reflect the shape of a half moon. That was the spot where the great Apache Warrior Geronimo had hidden the gold. The spot was on the northwest side of the burned post, east of Colossal Cave, where the river curved away from the mountain and took the shape of a snake. I climbed to the top of this particular mountain numerous times before sunrise, by myself. Once I took my five and seven-year-old sisters. For making my sisters a part of the expedition, my parents gave me a thorough spanking. Of course, at the time I felt their actions were tremendously unjustified.

Another time, during a full moon, I took my father. It took a surprising amount of convincing. This surprised me a little. Didn't he like gold? He stayed with me on the mountaintop for over an hour, and I learned much from him that night. He spoke to me about life and the importance of taking care of the family and being well educated. He wanted me to go to college so we could start a business. I found treasure after all that night, although it wasn't the treasure I had expected. This experience with my father on the mountain was worth all the gold I could ever find in a lifetime.

The story of how Geronimo got the gold in the first place is not a pleasant one. Geronimo and his warriors took the gold from a stagecoach post between Tombstone and Tucson in the 1800s. According to the story, he killed everyone on the scene and burned down the post. The post had been located on the ranch's property about three hundred yards northeast of the lake. The burned ruins could still be seen when I lived there. I spent a great deal of my time during that summer looking for that gold. Whenever Willy, a school friend of mine from nearby *Rancho del Lago*, would come over to visit me, we would go treasure hunting and had a great time. Willy and I were a combination of Tom

Sawyer and Huckleberry Finn, only far away from the cool and green of the Mississippi. Our adventures took place in the hot mountains of Arizona.

The rest of 1963 went by fast. 1964 also went by too quickly. We were getting close to the end of my first school year at Vail Elementary School District No. 20. I had learned quite a bit of English during my first year thanks to a special, kind, and gentle teacher who spent her lunch hour with me every day. She was very demanding. My beloved Mrs. Braun would give me a great deal of homework every day, except for weekends. She was putting all of her heart into the instruction so I would learn English quickly. I still remember her well. She was a beautiful person. She was my sister's third-grade teacher and my fifth-grade reading instructor. She was a woman of roughly sixty years who spoke German, Japanese, and three other languages. She taught me a great deal about discipline, responsibility, freedom, democracy, fair play, the Constitution, and above all, loving the United States. When my two sisters and I matriculated in Pima County, I was placed in the fifth grade. I was actually at an eighth grade level in math and science but was held back since I could not speak English.

Mrs. Braun visited our family at the ranch occasionally on weekends to check on our English. She would drive twenty-two miles from Tucson, where she lived, just to go over a few lessons with us on Saturday morning. She knew that we would be moving to California the following year, and she wanted us to be well prepared for our new school in the Golden State. We left Arizona in early July 1964. Ten years later in 1974, Mrs. Braun and her daughter attended my sister Ana's wedding in California. That was the last time I saw her. Mrs. Braun has always occupied a special place in my heart.

In early 1964 my father traded his 1956 Chevy Bel Air for a light-green 1960 Rambler, and he taught me to handle the steering wheel. I couldn't reach the gas pedal yet. At this time we were preparing to leave for California. We would leave once we finished our school year. By April we had moved into the big house with the Burrises. My father was tailoring and repairing the highway patrolmen's uniforms at home and would deliver them, when ready, to a Broadway store in Tucson. I believe that the company had hired him on a part-time basis four months previously. During those months, the chain store offered him a full-time job, and my parents talked about possibly staying in Arizona and moving to Tucson to live. "We could have good opportunities in Tucson," he would tell my mother constantly. They spoke about that decision for several months, and they asked for my opinion on numerous occasions. I had met several kids from California who were visiting the Colossal Cave, and they spoke about the wonders of their home state. Their parents also told me that California was a nice place to live and that it was filled with opportunities. A few parents gave me their business cards or telephone numbers so that I could call them once we arrived there in case we needed help. Other families from Colorado, Nevada, and Oregon also invited us to move to their states. A couple of tourists even visited *La Posta Quemada* Ranch to speak with my parents and offer them a job if we moved to their state. Their comments, good hearts, and generosity influenced me tremendously, and I persuaded my parents to move to California. The time had come for us to depart. I interpreted for my parents as they thanked Mr. Burris and Susanita for helping us.

Susanita told me, "You must do well in school and go on to college. I will visit you all someday in California to see how you are doing in school." She kissed me on the forehead and waved good-bye. Her eyes were filled with tears as my father started up the engine. She visited us three years later. We were living in Oxnard and I was in the eighth grade. Mr. Burris also visited us in Oxnard when I was in high school. He gave me several twenty-dollar bills in a gold clip for my graduation. And he told me how happy he was to have sponsored our journey to the United States. I told him I was getting ready for college and he said that he was proud of me. That was the last time I saw him.

California

It took us several weeks to reach our destination—Ventura, California. On the way, we stayed in Chula Vista for two weeks. My father and his younger brother, a diesel mechanic who lived there, repaired our car by replacing half the engine. We arrived in Ventura a week later.

The rest of the 1964 summer, I went to work with my parents, harvesting strawberries in Oxnard. My two sisters and I attended Driffill Elementary

School, where Mr. Sal Craven, my sixth-grade teacher, would ask me to compete with an adding machine in computing multiplication tables. Beating that piece of technology to the right answer did wonders for my self-confidence. Mr. Craven was a great influence in my young life. At the same time I was going to school, I started working at a mom-and-pop store where Mexican food, bread, and other items were sold. *La Perla Mexican Tortilla Factory* was its name. We lived behind the business in a three-room house in the middle of town. Our building was surrounded by businesses. I remember walking into *La Perla* soon after we were settled in Oxnard and asking the owner, Mr. Valeriano Sanchez, if he needed someone to help him in the store. He told me to return later that afternoon, and his wife Luicita, a petite lady in her mid-sixties, hired me. Her dark, black hair was now almost half white. She was always cooking Mexican food. That particular afternoon, she was cooking chicken enchiladas with red sauce and offered me a couple. After I finished eating, she showed me what I was supposed to do. Every day after school, I was to clean the bakery room and the 106 aluminum trays on which the Mexican bread was baked. I started that moment. I cleaned those trays six days a week after school, except Tuesday, for a year and a half. I was paid six dollars per week. I confess that I was happy with my job.

After several months, they asked me if I wanted to work in the front of the store, and Bobby, the Sanchez's twenty-eight-year-old son, taught me my responsibilities. After a while, I was also waiting on customers, and my pay was raised to $1.15 per hour. I worked eighteen to twenty hours every weekend and more hours during the summer. I worked there from sixth grade until my junior year in high school. *La Perla* gave me my first practical management experience. I was responsible for the factory many times, working in tandem with my employers. I managed the store and was responsible for five other adult employees, including my father. The Mexican bread, tortillas, and other products were delivered to different chain stores and several restaurants in Ventura, Santa Barbara, and Los Angeles counties every day. I was making $32.00 per week during the summer, a great deal of money for a fourteen-year-old boy. I felt rich, and I had learned to appreciate the value of money.

When I was temporary laid off in the summer of 1966, I went to harvest grapes in nearby Bakersfield and made close to $600.00 that summer. That was hard work. I had to get up at five in the morning. I started working in the fields at seven, often putting in ten hours a day if not more. This harshness of the job confirmed my commitment to school. I was absolutely resolved to go to college. I knew that the only way to accomplish my dreams was by being well-prepared through education. I was asked to return to work at *La Perla* in September for a few more years and later worked at McDonald's.

In the summer of 1968, I met Robert Kennedy. I was sixteen when he visited Oxnard during his campaign in California. It was a beautiful, warm afternoon, and a cool sea breeze was blowing Mr. Kennedy's hair. He was constantly fixing it with his left hand. I was thrilled to encounter a man of his stature. Mr. Kennedy impressed me tremendously. He radiated passion, caring, and true commitment to people when he spoke. He was visiting with the people in town and answering questions after giving a brief talk. I remember that he walked toward me, placed his right hand on my shoulder, and asked me, "How are you doing in school, young man?"

"Fine, sir, thank you," I responded.

He continued to meet with people. I observed how he spoke, in a soft voice, to an elder citizen wanting to touch him. He then said something to the effect that everyone should get an education. He looked back at me and said, "Continue doing well in school," squeezed my shoulder with his right hand, smiled, and walked away toward the intersection of B and Fifth Street, away from the kiosk where he had spoken. As he made his way back to his caravan, he continued talking and shaking people's hands. He was driven away on Fifth Street heading for Los Angeles.

I distributed pamphlets in Oxnard for his candidacy during those days. He was assassinated several days thereafter at the Ambassador Hotel in Los Angeles. I cried that day and remembered the assassinations of his brother, Robert Kennedy, and Dr. Martin Luther King.

I did well throughout my elementary and high school years, and my parents were very proud of me. At this time in my life, I was fortunate to have mentors who set my feet firmly on the path to success. I had teachers who truly cared for my education and constantly encouraged me—teachers like Mrs. Braun, in Vail, Arizona; Mr. Craven at Driffill Elementary School; and Mrs. Story, a 6'3" woman of Russian descent who was a firm disciplinarian. She was strict, but some students knew she cared for all of us and that her greatest concern was for us to learn well in her English class at Haydock Junior High.

Then there was Mr. Willard Appenzeller, my counselor at Oxnard High School. I was unfairly placed in remedial classes during my freshman year, and he fought for two years to have me placed in college prep courses, which actually matched my skill level. I remember Mr. Steffan Nyarady, my algebra teacher, whom I assisted as an aide tutoring the students who were behind in his class; and Mr. Miller, another one of my math teachers, who said to me, "Honorable men never give up and never become quitters; they always fight for their honor and for what they believe. Although you may have many obstacles, never give up." His words have always been on my mind.

At the top of my list are Mrs. Jean Folkes, Mr. Richard Laidlaw, and Mr. Charles Dunn, the varsity basketball coach and history teacher. Whenever I saw him on campus, he would ask me if I was getting ready for my SAT test. He steered me out of trouble during my four years in high school. I sometimes think about all the unnecessary suffering that would be cured in this world if there were more men like Mr. Dunn. He constantly encouraged me to continue achieving in athletics and education. What was very important about all these praiseworthy and honorable human beings was that they all sincerely meant what they said to me. How could I have betrayed the trust of so many people committed to my life's success? I would have been a fraud to them if I had dropped out of school. From the bottom of my heart I say thank you to them and to all the other unsung heroes in this world.

With the greatest pride I became a US citizen on July 31, 1970. One of my best friends in high school, Michael Yatabe, became my witness. Throughout my school years, I had been fairly popular. I was well liked and was always called by competing parties if there was going to be a brawl after school. I was a peacemaker. I had taken karate and judo since the sixth grade and also practiced boxing. I excelled in these sports. My father taught me to box, and he had practiced with me periodically since I was a child. I knew how to defend myself and used my skills to break up fights on several occasions in junior high and high school, although I am only 5'6". My classmates respected me.

I played baseball during the summer whenever I could. This wasn't as often as I would have liked since I was employed full-time. I also played during my four years at Oxnard High. In my 1971 high school yearbook, it reads near my photo, "Miguel sparked the team on center and had a .400 batting average." We became the Marmonte League Champions in 1971. I received two baseball offers from scouts who visited me at home, and I was invited to try out in the minors after graduating from high school. I was torn. I had scored high on my SAT test and had been notified by Senator Omer L. Rains' office that I had won a California State Scholarship. Eventually I decided that as much as I loved baseball, my education was paramount. I registered at Ventura Community College.

My plan was to attend UC Hastings, College of Law, after graduating from college, but in the meantime, I had decided to stay in a community college near home for my first two years. My parents needed me. My father was very ill; he was expected to live two years, maybe less. When I enrolled in college, the pride he showed in me acted as a great spur to my efforts.

"Honorable men never give up and never become quitters; they always fight for their honor and for what they believe. Although you may have many obstacles, never give up."

CHAPTER 4

Years in College

—— ••• ——

Our duty, as men and women, is to proceed as if limits to our ability did
not exist. We are collaborators in creation.

Pierre Teilhard de Chardin

I got involved in politics for the time in my life while attending Ventura
Community College in 1971-'73. I felt changes needed to be made in student
government and in the college's policy toward the diverse people who attended it.
This was especially true in regard to the obtuse attitudes of one or two professors
and many students who, possibly through their ignorance of different cultures,
thought that they knew the absolute truth. Really they were just giving expression
to their xenophobic beliefs. I felt that I could help make the changes needed on
campus, and I wanted to be part of this new process. I felt that I could convince

the students—Chicanos, Latinos, Afro Americans, Anglo Americans, Asian Americans, Native Americans, and others—to work together as a team without self-interest. The new student board was going to make decisions to benefit the whole student population. We were not going to cheat anybody via a hidden agenda or act with malicious intent, arrogance, or unethical actions. I did not like politics because I was a quiet person and did not want to be in the spotlight, but I was compelled to speak out then, as I am now, whenever I saw discrimination practiced against anyone.

Ventura Community College had excellent professors. Mr. Desmond Jones, an English political science professor, had emigrated to the United States. We conversed often outside of class. He continuously encouraged me to get involved in student politics because I had a good mind for grasping political concepts and was good in a debate. I told him that I did not know anything about politics, but maybe it was a good idea to become involved. I felt I had to defend myself frequently as a "minority". To this day, I do not agree with the term because I am first and foremost an American, or more precisely, a Mexican American, as we are labeled for political reasons. What in the world is a "minority" anyway? According to our political system, I am an American, and I have one vote like every other citizen. The term "minority" seems hopelessly outdated to me, or used for social-political purposes.

Racism: A serious issue.

During one of our lunchtime conversations, I told Professor Jones that I had witnessed a few racist actions or comments made in the past toward Chicano or Black friends in high school and during the first weeks of the semester in college, but these experiences had been very subtle. They would not have been provable in a court of law. Mr. Jones responded, "That's why you should learn to present your arguments more convincingly concerning the dynamics of might versus right, power versus authority, [and] freedom versus liberty." More than simply asking us to memorize facts and excel on tests, Professor Jones taught us to think and carefully analyze our arguments. He and another instructor, Professor Ray Reyes, showed us how to present our arguments with precise foundations, not just rhetoric. I remember how stirring it was to hear Professor

Reyes tell us in class, "You must defend your rights. Fight for justice and for what you believe in. We are a nation of immigrants and have equal rights." I attempt to live up to his words every day of my life.

On several occasions, I had been told to go back to wherever I came from by fellow students. Worse was an eye-opening experience I had in class when a professor whom I admired for his political, economic, and historical knowledge said, "All Mexicans should go back to wherever they came from." I was tremendously embarrassed. I was at a loss for words. I did not want to be disrespectful, but at the same time I wanted to give my thoughts about his racist comment. I remember in that moment being aware of how young and naïve I was. Suddenly, Dennis, an Anglo student with long hair and a beard, spoke up. He dressed like a hippie and was a Vietnam veteran. With intense, silent gratitude I heard him defend me with eloquent and passionate words that were both assertive and respectful.

When class was over, the instructor approached me and apologized. However, that racist incident and others involving students, along with Professors Jones and Reyes's persistent encouragement for me to get involved in student politics, influenced me to run for the position of student body vice president. Maybe this way, I told myself, I could help correct those wrongs that still existed on campus. The prejudice I faced at Ventura College, in addition to the bad experiences I had endured in high school, left me with no alternative. I suddenly recalled the humiliation of being placed in remedial classes as a high school freshman instead of college prep courses. A high school math teacher had told me that Mexicans belonged in those classes.

I was voted in as vice president, and within a few months I had become a very outspoken person. I turned into a student who wanted to change peoples' minds about different cultures, especially those who were racist, or people with narrow-minded views.

After I won the election, I met with John, an Anglo American, five or six years older than I. He was the student body president, and we had long conversations about our different platforms. "We can work together and do a good job," he said. "I hate to admit it, but I grew up thinking that you guys were different from us. My parents used to tell me that Mexicans were nothing but troublemakers. When I came to college, I found out that you are hardworking people with the same dreams we have, and we have no real differences. I'm starting to see how prejudiced my parents are. They brought me up to be like them, to dislike Mexicans and Blacks. I wish they could see how wrong they are."

I served as the Ventura Community College Student Body Vice President and then became the treasurer. I felt more comfortable as treasurer and was able to become more involved in student government in this position. I was also elected president of *MECHA* (Mexican & Chicano Student Association). I played baseball as a freshman but soon decided it was more important to dedicate myself to my studies. I dedicated most of my time to studying, pouring over books for four to five hours in the library every day. I followed this same schedule for the rest of my college years. I searched for good causes to occupy whatever free time I had available. I became involved with social activist Cesar Chavez and accompanied him on several marches and strikes in Oxnard, Delano, Bakersfield, Fresno, and other cities, demanding social justice for the migrant workers. I learned a great deal from Mr. Chavez and was inspired by his true sense of social justice.

I also worked with students in my college and with farm workers in the area, an invaluable practical experience that later helped me as a manager and consultant in multinational organizations. I became a PEER counselor assisting incoming students at Ventura College. We had excellent groups of students serving in MECHA and on the student board. Together we taught English and math to children from many parts of the world. We led voter registration campaigns throughout Ventura County.

In the early seventies, immigrants were strongly classified as subservient by many ignorant, racist people. They derided us as "the trouble maker Mexicans," or "wet backs" and were especially cruel when we spoke out for our rights. Sadly and shamefully, this attitude still prevails today among people in many parts of the country I have visited.

We had set an objective that was not easy, and that was to persuade as many families as possible from Ventura County to send their young adult children to college. They instead wanted them to work. We embarked on a long and hard endeavor. We had a specific goal, well-thought-out strategies, a team, and the motivation and the will to get more students to register in college. We succeeded tremendously in those two years. There were many of us, like my close friend, Arnulfo Casillas, Ricardo Walker, Alfonso Gonzalez, Luisa, Mary, Jorge "George" Valle, Luis, Ruben, Pete Juarez, and Carmen Cartwright, to name a few. We worked hard to guarantee that future students would get a better education.

As student representatives of our college, four of us attended the Student Body Associations of California Junior Colleges Convention in Anaheim to discuss issues relevant to junior college students in California. We went in with many positive proposals. We worked thousands of hours to achieve our objectives, with the guidance of our professors and advisors at the college like the late Ray Reyes, John Woolley, Isiah "Bubba" Brown, Rene Rodriguez, and my dear professor and friend the late Peter Drucker. We worked hard in those two years. After graduating from junior college in June 1973 with an Associate of Arts, I was accepted at the University of California, Santa Barbara (UCSB).

Then tragedy struck. My father was killed in a bus accident the summer of '73 along with forty-two other people. He was visiting his parents in Mexico. I never got the chance to say farewell to him. My mother asked me to drop out of college so I could work. It was a painful decision, but I eventually refused to quit school. We buried my father with great pain, which I still feel to this day.

I got engaged that same summer to my girlfriend, Tina. Both of our families had met in Sonora when we were children, in 1959. Tina and I met again later while I was a sophomore in college. We got married in 1976 and have been married ever since.

During my first year at the beautiful UCSB campus by the sea in Goleta, California, I had a lot of hard work to do. I was the receptionist at the Chicano Studies Department and a PEER counselor during the summer. And I continued in the Chicano Student Association, volunteering in tutoring young children at different elementary schools in Goleta and the Santa Barbara area. Everything went well on campus the first year. I only had time for studying, working, and doing volunteer assignments for the children four hours per week.

In the first quarter, I met Willy, a classmate who was in his early forties. He was a quiet, husky man who always sat next to me in the front of the classroom. We had three classes together. After a few weeks, we became friends. He always asked me if I was doing well in class. Willy had gotten a low grade on our first partial public administration exam. I told him that I would tutor him, and he accepted, so we spent time together between classes and studied. Willy tried to persuade me to double major because I was constantly asking questions in a sociology class that I enjoyed very much. The class's professor was always complimenting me for my responses. He was a young Ph.D. from England who was visiting our campus for a year. He had become very popular with his theories about deviant behavior. I told Willy that I had a heavy load of classes, thus I did not think that I would do well with a double major. Dr. Donald R. Cressey, a sociology professor whom I highly respected at UCSB, influenced me to make my decision.

Before the quarter was over, I had enrolled in the Criminal Justice Certificate Program. This certification later helped me to get my first job as a police officer, a profession I loved. Willy was a good man and spoke to me as though he were my father. I always listened carefully to his advice. He had been going to school for years. I eventually found out that he had been incarcerated. Willy was in a special program for prisoners in which they did the first two years of college in prison. Then, if they earned the honor, they could attend a university nearby. He told me he had been transferred to Lompoc Prison in Santa Maria from Texas years prior. He seemed genuinely sorry for what he had done. "I made a mistake as a young man, and I'm paying for it," he said. Willy was driven to the UCSB campus every day at 8:00 a.m. and had to be on the bus by 5:00 p.m. If he was a minute late, all the privileges would be revoked and he would not be able to continue attending the university.

A few weeks before our graduation, Willy told me that he cared for me very much and appreciated my friendship. "I regret what I did when I was a young man, and I want you to be a good citizen and do well." I was surprised that he was talking so seriously that day. We talked for about two hours, and he said that he wanted me to know the truth about him because I had trusted him in the two years since we had become friends. We had several classes together. He told me about a terrible day that had occurred many years ago. "I got home early from work and found my wife with another man." He stopped to compose himself. I waited quietly. He continued, "I went crazy. I loved my wife very much, and I killed them both." We were silent for a minute, and I hugged him. I walked with him to his bus. He embraced me and got on. I kept my eyes on him until he sat down and looked at me. He waved good-bye and yelled, as the bus was driving away, "I want you to be a good man." I smiled and waved good-bye. I never saw him again. Willy's strength in motivating people, his genuine gratitude toward those who helped him, his positivity about life, and his passion to help other inmates become better citizens showed me that he had a good heart and had truly repented for what he had done. Willy was an inspiration to me.

My senior year at UCSB continued to be a tough grind. I studied hard every evening from 6:30 p.m. to 12:00 a.m. in a cubicle for graduate students on the top floor in the campus library. I kept my grades up in order to maintain my state scholarship. I was also getting more involved with events on campus, such as representing our organization at times when speaking with the chancellor or vice chancellor and coordinating with other student association representatives about issues affecting Chicanos. I took extra summer courses and numerous seminars during the school year. I was getting ready to graduate in June of 1975. I did not want to stay a day longer in school than I had to because I had many plans for my future.

I continued with my academic preparation and job responsibilities. By this time, I had become a much-disciplined person and had gained my first insights of wisdom. I grew to know my strengths and weaknesses. I knew how to study wisely and how to work hard.

One afternoon the Chicano Student Association president called the Chicano students in to discuss a problem. He had received a telephone call from a friend at the governor's office, Edmond Brown, stating that the chancellor, Vernon Cheadle, was attempting to cut off scholarships to "minority" students. We were incensed. The leaders discussed our position among some of the members of the association, and after a debate we finally decided to take a stand against the chancellor's decision. We marched in solidarity against the administration building. It was a hot afternoon, about 3:30 p.m., when we surrounded the building. Students from other organizations that were also going to be affected joined in: The Native-American Student Association, The Black-Student Association, and about thirty Anglo students who sympathized with us. We protested in front of the administration and made a human chain. We refused to allow anybody in or out of the building until the chancellor spoke with us. We were told that chancellor Cheadle was away from the campus, so the vice chancellor attempted to represent him, but to no avail. We chanted in unison, "We want Cheadle!" At around 5:00 p.m., more police officers arrived and stood by. Some students were yelling, "Do they want another Kent State?"

I was growing worried. Arnulfo approached me and whispered in my ear that he thought it was time to leave. He did not want me to get into any trouble. "Things are going to be nasty here," he said. I knew what he was capable of doing. Arnulfo was a Vietnam veteran who had escaped death many times during the war. His scars proved it. I remember abruptly waking him up during an all-night strike with Cesar Chavez in Ventura County during our junior college protests, and his swift, automatic, reaction almost cost me my life. Arnulfo approached me and said, "I want you to get out of here! This is going to get serious!" I was troubled. I had seen Arnulfo speaking to other Vietnam veteran students, and they meant business. They were speaking about getting into the computer room and sabotaging the whole UC system. I left the area.

The following morning the student's university newspaper, *The Daily Nexus*, reported on the front page that several students had been arrested. They were eventually pardoned. This demonstration and other protests saved the scholarship program. A few weeks later, at graduation, Chancellor Cheadle saw me and other students after taking our graduation oath. He approached me and said,

"Congratulations, you have done a good job. We had our differences, but that's part of a student's life learning process. You have a great potential to do many things. Good luck." We took a photograph together and said good-bye with a handshake.

Experimenting With Marijuana

If you wondered whether or not I ever took drugs during my high school or college years, as my peers were constantly doing, I was never interested. However, my curiosity was stronger than my disinterest. I smoked two joints one night when I was a senior at UCSB, and that was enough for me to decide that I could enjoy life without drugs. I realized during that experience that I was incapable of controlling my body. As I walked to my dorm, my body seemed to be going in slow motion. In fact, as I attempted to go up a stairway, I had to crawl to get to my living quarters on the second floor of my San Rafael dorm. I was conscious about what I was doing, yet my mind felt as though I was floating. Yes, I could think clearly; I was conscious of my actions, and everything in movement—my hands, my feet as I walked—seemed to be in slow motion.

"I am an idiot?" I thought. "This is what people take drugs for?" I was upset with myself. I had seen too many students on campus under the influence of all types of drugs who took them just to feel high. They acted very foolishly, or sometimes they were aggressive. Some of them looked spaced out. Their attitude got worse when drugs were mixed with alcohol—they appeared to be out of touch with reality, and many behaved as imbeciles. But most disheartening, I saw several friends slowly deteriorate into mental disorders resulting from their drug use, eventually dropping out of college. I witnessed too many people pass out and go into a coma, or a dear friend die in college due to an overdose. I was certain that drugs and alcohol were not going to be part of my life.

I graduated on June 17, 1975, with a BA in Political Science and a Criminal Justice Certificate. That same morning, I moved out of my dorm. I had only twenty dollars in my pocket. I needed a job. I also wanted to start getting ready for the LSAT so I could continue on to law school. I returned to Oxnard that same day. The following week, I started harvesting strawberries. I was waiting for job interviews. I had applied with several companies, including McDonald's, Procter & Gamble, and the City of Oxnard. I even drove four hours to the San Francisco area to take an exam for a law enforcement position, but it was too far, and I did not really want to leave Oxnard. My mother still needed me near. I had also taken a test for the Air Force, but I was not enthusiastic about either of the exams. I took the test distractedly, filling in the spaces without reading most of the questions. I did not want to leave my town. My mother and I were very close but could not live together; she had remarried, and her new husband did not like me at all. He was an Anglo American attorney who had worked as a judge in Santa Barbara County. Our views constantly clashed, and he was continually bothering my mother about our relationship. He did not want her to be close to me. He was arrogant and offensive at times, and she always felt the need to apologize for his rudeness and bad manners. I had to swallow my pride for my mother's peace of mind. A few weeks after my graduation, he wrote me a letter telling me to stay away from my mother. I never understood the source of his great animosity toward me.

My mother, my two sisters, and I had been a close family since my father's death, and he had come from two failed marriages. My mom had asked me not to move away from the area. She needed me to stay near her. She had lost my father two years before, and now she did not want to lose her son. After my father was killed, she had isolated herself in her bedroom for months and lost a great deal of weight. She was losing her will to live. I had no choice. I was determined to do what I could for her and so complied with her wish to stay in the area. My younger sister, Anabel, had married her high school boyfriend, Joe. He was in the Air Force. They lived in Panama City, Florida. When I returned to Oxnard from UCSB, my mother had asked me to take care of my youngest sister, Lily, who was sixteen. Lily moved in with me, and I was grateful for her company. I was a bit lonely. I missed my girlfriend, who was finishing her university degree in Mexico.

Approximately six weeks after graduating, while I was working in Oxnard and considering my future, a well-dressed man in an expensive suit found me working in a strawberry field. He asked me if I wanted to work on a special research project funded by the state of California. They needed a person with university certification and criminal justice knowledge. He had read an essay about criminal behavior and prevention that I had written for Professor Donald Cressey's criminology classes at UCSB, and his team felt that I was the person they needed to assist in the project. I was very excited and responded yes before he had even finished telling me about the job. The following Monday, I reported to the City of Oxnard personnel department and was hired for a six-month funded project. I was taken to the police department, which was adjacent to city hall, and introduced to the chief of police, Robert P. Owens. My job was to research the different problems that existed within the Ventura County justice system as it attempted to meet the needs of diverse races.

While doing my research, I was fortunate enough to meet excellent law enforcement officers who wholeheartedly believed in what they were doing, men like Chief Robert P. Owens, Sergeant Denny Phillips, Detective Merle Dove, Detective Sgt. Lee Monahan, Lieutenant Jim Latimer, Officers Carlos E. Noriega, Dennis Pete, Steve Hendrix, Fred Jackson, Gene Thayer, and, in particular, my friend and training officer, the late Officer Robert Stofey and his wife Gayle. They assisted me tremendously in making the next transition in my life. I was going to become a police officer.

CHAPTER 5

A Cop in California

All men and women are created equal under our Constitution

After meeting Oxnard's chief of police, Robert P. Owens, I was welcomed into the program in the summer of 1975. I was introduced to the man in charge of the research project, Mr. McCallum, who gave me all the details about my part in the research. He spent most of the day with me discussing his objectives for the project and then left me alone to do the research in my own way at the Oxnard Police Department, the district attorney's office, and the court system. He asked me to prepare a weekly report and discuss my findings with him, but we only met twice after our first meeting. Oxnard was a city of about eighty-five thousand people and had approximately 102 police officers in a community that was about 32 percent Hispanic, 15 percent Black, 48 percent Anglo, and 5 percent Asian.

During the early stages of my research, I reported to Detective Merle Dove. He taught me about the criminal justice process. I started with the district attorney's office, public defender's office, and the police department. Detective Dove was a large, middle-aged man who chain-smoked, and was well mannered and honest. The first day I met him, he told me that he was a detective and was substituting for the court liaison officer, Fred Estrella, who was on vacation. Dove told me that he would answer any questions I might have. "This type of project," he said, "will help us do better police work and will make us aware of the many problems we need to resolve." I listened very carefully to everything he said and asked many questions, which he was always gracious enough to answer.

For the duration of the daily drives we took to the courthouse in Ventura, Dove would tell me stories about his time on the force. I especially remember a story he told about the time he almost got shot during a high-speed pursuit. "A bullet came through the windshield," he told me. "It hit this ring." He made a fist with his right hand and showed me a heavy ring on his ring finger. "The bullet ricocheted away from my body and hit the car seat between my legs. This ring saved my life." He took the ring off and handed it to me. The ring was heavy, and its golden-yellow surface had dulled slightly with age. It had been repaired, but there was a noticeable flaw on the spot where the bullet had hit.

Detective Dove had also been involved in a case where an Oxnard officer was slain. It took him some time to return to his former self. "All of us are affected psychologically, one way or another," he said, "When an officer is killed. This isn't like most jobs. We can't afford to make any mistakes, or we're dead." He paused for a moment. "Being a cop isn't easy. There are people out there who want to hurt us. You can never let your guard down. Years ago the Hell's Angels and other biker groups were riding around California. One of their tests to become a member of the gang was to kill a cop."

Dove taught me about observation and interviewing techniques. I spent several weeks with him, during which we became friends. We often spoke about different police procedures and personal matters. Sometime later, when I was a rookie patrolman, he became my supervisor and told me to be wary of some people on the force. "Just be careful with two or three of these guys," he said. "They have something against you because you're well educated. Never be outspoken with them because they can get you in trouble. Just continue to do a good job and follow the rules, and you'll be okay." He gave me this advice while I was performing my evaluation two years into my career at Oxnard PD. Detective Dove passed of cardiac arrest a few months after the evaluation. He was an admirable man, the grandfather everyone wants to have.

Three months into the program, I had almost finished my part of the research. By this time I had been assigned a desk in the Crime Prevention Unit. Chief Owens had asked me if I would assist the police officers in the CPU in helping Spanish-speaking citizens become aware of how the Crime Prevention Unit could help everyone in their community. While I was doing my research, the officers in the CPU invited me to assist them as a Spanish interpreter. I learned a great deal about police work from two of the unit's officers, my friends Larry Fryar and Darrel Ulmer, and from other detectives who had called me when they needed a Spanish interpreter during interrogations.

Due to the numerous problems the police department had with the Spanish-speaking community, an idea came to mind. I wanted to start a live radio program in which I would discuss police issues in Spanish. A few weeks into the research project, I started to co-host a radio talk show on KOXR, a local Spanish station. I spoke about crime prevention, drugs and their ill effects, immigration, politics, and police brutality, an important issue in the city during those years. Chief Owens loved the talk show; he was aware of everything we discussed. He told me on a few occasions that I had crossed some boundaries, but in general he liked my commentary and backed the program wholeheartedly. This was in spite of the fact that, as Chief Owens told me, a few high-brass officers were attempting to stop me. Chief Owens wanted to promote positive public relations with the Spanish-speaking community, and the show fit perfectly with this aspiration. Owens was a very progressive law enforcement administrator. He had innovative ideas that later became standards in law enforcement departments around the country, like computerizing crime reports, and report transcription eliminating hand written reports, crime analysis, and neighborhood-based policing.

During this time, and later, after I became a police officer, he asked me on numerous occasions to promote our department throughout the community. I made presentations at the Oxnard Elks Club and other places where I was invited. At times Chief Owens accompanied me, which, to my surprise, caused some problems with a few officers and lieutenants. What they saw as the chief's favoritism increased their dislike toward me as a person, or as a "Mexican," as some of them called me behind my back. They never made these statements to my face because I was well educated and they were afraid that I might file a grievance against them. They knew me too well and were certain that I would do whatever was necessary to achieve justice if I ever witnessed any racism or heard any prejudiced comments.

The radio program kept increasing in popularity in Ventura County. Eventually, it was heard in Santa Barbara and Los Angeles counties. I explained on the show that if any citizen ever saw me or any other police officer harassing or abusing our powers, it was their duty to file a grievance. I talked about how to file complaints against abusive officers, initiate lawsuits, and similar topics. Some officers disliked me for that. When an officer would ask me why I was discussing such topics on the air, I would tell him that it was a fact that some officers were abusive toward Blacks and Mexicans. I explained that if a citizen knew what to do when his or her rights were violated, it would help deter the problem. It worked.

Sgt. Denny Phillips was a quiet man who would speak only when he had a wise comment to make; otherwise he would just listen. He was in charge of the Crime Prevention Unit and was not liked much by some officers because they felt that his unit was not doing real police work. They called the officers in the CPU "the chief's pussy cats." In reality, Officers Fryar and Ulmer in the CPU were contributing a great deal to the community by offering speaking engagements about crime prevention and performing other special assignments with the citizenry. "There is far more to police work than simply making arrests; we have to educate citizens and some police officers," Fryar used to tell me. We take an oath when we become police officers to protect, serve, and defend every law-abiding citizen in our communities regardless of creed, race, or religious affiliation. Officer Fryar later became an investigator for the Ventura County District Attorney's office.

Police Reserve Officer

Later that same year, while I was doing my research, Sergeant Lee Monahan and Deputy Chief of Police Jack Snyder asked me several times if I wanted to become a reserve police officer. They could see that I loved what I was doing in the Crime Prevention Unit and on the radio show. I eagerly accepted. I passed both the written and oral exams and started attending the police academy in the evenings after work from 6:00 p.m. to 10:00 p.m. I underwent extensive and excruciating training at the Oxnard Reserve Police Academy. After three months, I graduated with about ten other reserve officer candidates. Deputy Chief Snyder was very happy that I had become a police reserve officer, and as I received my diploma from him at graduation, said, "I am very proud that you have become one of us, young man." He later invited me to lunch and told me what he expected from me. "Don't let me down, son. I believe in you and like what you have done with that radio show you have, even if it has caused a little hell at our station." As a police reserve officer, I usually volunteered every weekend during the mid-shift, from 4:00 p.m. to 2:00 a.m., and sometimes twice during the week. In the following eight months, I logged over five hundred hours.

The First Experience

It was sunny and breezy one Saturday afternoon in 1975 when I was riding with Officer Chatwin. We heard a call given to Charles 1, the unit assigned to the north end of town, Beat 1. "Charles 1, Charles 1," stated Nancy, the dispatcher.

"Go ahead," responded the officer.

"Possible 211 in progress at the 7-11 on Vineyard and 101; suspect white male, 5'9", blond hair, 180 pounds, wearing a red-and-white striped T-shirt, blue Levis.

"Charles 1. 10-4, responding from C Street and Gonzalez," answered the officer.

"Charles 1. Suspect just left the scene on a black dirt motorcycle, northbound on Vineyard," said the dispatcher.

"10-4," responded Charles 1.

Officer Chatwin, my partner, grabbed the mike and said, "Charles 3, copied. We'll back up." As we were driving to the scene of the possible robbery, a motorcyclist fitting the robber's description rode into view from an adjacent street in front of our unit. Officer Chatwin asked the dispatcher to confirm the description of the suspect, and as she was about to finish, my partner exclaimed, "That's him!" He turned the unit's red light on and started his pursuit of the suspect. My pulse immediately started racing. I grabbed the mike and said, "Charles 3, in pursuit of robbery suspect."

"10-4," responded the dispatcher.

We chased the suspect for about a mile as he zigzagged between cars. We were driving toward Saticoy, a small town east of Oxnard. The traffic was slower in that area. I was updating our location when, suddenly, the motorcyclist made a sharp left turn. We followed, barely keeping the police unit on the road, and chased him for another half mile.

The motorcyclist rode into a lemon orchard. Unfortunately for him the lemon orchard was closed in with a chain-link fence. We continued our pursuit, racing in and out between the lemon trees. A heavy cloud of dust picked up as a result. We were about fifty yards away when I asked my partner to stop the car. I told him to keep following in the car and I would attempt to cut the suspect off as he tried to ride out of the field. I got out of the unit and quickly and carefully observed the situation. The motorcyclist reached the fence at the end of the field. He made a quick right turn. I ran to toward the south fence, stopped after about thirty yards, and squatted. I was trying to see if the suspect had continued riding the motorcycle or had ditched his vehicle and gone over the fence. I saw that he was still riding. He was heading along the fence, coming toward me fast. "I got you," I thought. I ran toward the fence and dove into the air. I knocked him off the motorcycle and then hooked my right arm around his neck after he stood up. I pulled him to the ground and subdued him.

Within a minute, Officer Chatwin arrived. "You okay?" he asked as he handcuffed the suspect. "Of course," I replied. I was shaking with adrenaline. My uniform was covered with dust. My partner placed the suspect in the back of the unit, and another officer who had arrived at the scene impounded the motorcycle. When I got back in the unit, my partner was smiling.

"We've done a great job. I'm proud of you!" he said.
"Thank you," I responded.

"I'm going to take you back to the station so you can get cleaned up," he said.

"Yeah," I said, looking at my battered uniform. "That sounds like a good idea."

As I cleaned up at the station, Officer Chatwin wrote the report, and then we returned to our patrol.

I stayed home the following day, Sunday. Soreness invaded every inch of my body. I had pulled a neck muscle, and I placed hot compresses on it all day. On Monday morning, when I arrived to work at the police station, the officers were treating me differently. As I was walking down the hallway toward my office, an officer who had never spoken to me previously said, "Good job, Miguel!" Two more officers were walking toward their units, and one of them said, "You're riding with me next weekend, partner." The other said, "The hell he is. He'll be with me. I have seniority." Finally–acceptance.

Another time, while patrolling on a Saturday morning, I was riding with one of the finest men I had met, Officer Armando "Mando" Ramirez, and we saw a suspect being chased in the park by two patrol units. The suspect, a drug user under the influence, was running through Colonia Park. We joined the pursuit, and when my partner and I saw the suspect coming our way, I got out of the patrol unit and ran after him. We ran in between project houses and through a house where two elderly citizens were watching television. I finally caught up to him, dove from behind, and knocked the suspect down. I hit my knees on the edge of the sidewalk; that prevented me from getting up quickly. We struggled, and I dropped my baton. He got up quickly and picked it up. I lay on the sidewalk looking up at him. He raised the baton in his right hand. He was moments away from cracking my skull open. At that same instant, I took my weapon from my holster, pointed it at him, and yelled, "Don't move at all, or I'll blow your balls off!" The suspect immediately dropped the baton and started running again. But Officer Steve Hendricks and his reserve officer arrived in their unit and caught him only a few yards away. "I came within a second or two of having my skull bashed in," I thought. I remembered Detective Dove's words. He was right. This wasn't like most jobs.

I was gaining the respect and trust of other officers. From the day that I took down the motorcycle suspect forward, I was a trusted reserve officer. More than a few officers asked me if I was coming to ride the following weekend and asked if I could be their partner. Five or six months passed, and the City of Oxnard posted a notice for three police officer openings. The chief of police asked me if I was going to take the test, and I responded affirmatively. "I'm glad. I expected you to join us. I've heard positive reports about you from several officers, and we want you to be on the force. Good luck," he said.

I had been preparing for the examination over the course of several months. I was well prepared when the time arrived. I took the oral test a month or so after the written test. On Saturday, the day of the written test, I arrived at the community center where it was being administered. Close to one thousand people showed up on that sunny morning; they had journeyed from all over the country to take the test. After a few weeks had passed, I received a notification card by mail informing me that I was number two on the list for the police officer position.

By now, I had been working for the Ventura Police Department as a community service officer for about nine months. I was also teaching at Oxnard

College and had a weekend management position in a mom-and-pop store called Thrifty Way Market. I needed to save money because I was planning to get married that year. I had four different jobs simultaneously in 1976. I married my girlfriend on December 18, 1976. Two weeks after returning from our honeymoon in Hawaii, I was hired by the City of Oxnard and attended the Sheriff and Police Academy for training.

Those were long, hard months. When we were allowed to go out on patrol, on weekends, I received training from excellent officers like Dennis Pete, Carlos E. Noriega, and Claude Robillard. I had actually ridden with them before when I was a police reserve officer. I was enchanted with my job and took it seriously. I strongly believed in the words all the new officers recite at graduation:

> I swear an oath to protect and serve society; law and order
> must be preserved in spite of the acts of any man.

After graduating from the academy, I was assigned for training to excellent officers whom I admired, like John Ahearn, Mike Alford, Tom Cady, Fred Jackson, and Carlos E. Noriega. I was later assigned to Officer Robert Stofey for two months. We were together almost fourteen hours a day, four days a week. I had to hand write our crime reports after our shift, or sometimes we had breakfast together. We were assigned to the morning shift, 9 p.m. to 7 a.m., Thursday through Sunday. Stofey was an exceptional officer. We ate, drank, and talked about police procedures and how to act in many hypothetical cases or special circumstances. We discussed how we would act if the other got ambushed or shot.

Stofey was constantly testing me about police procedures and real police case scenarios. He was 42 and a highly ethical and responsible man. An Oxnard Police veteran, Stofey hailed from New Jersey and had been in the Air Force as a young man. He taught me many things about human nature. By the time I had finished my training with Stofey, we were so close that I had picked up his Jersey accent. He was a lover of astronomy and enjoyed reading about the possibilities of extraterrestrial life, topics we discussed extensively during our ten-hour shifts.

Week One: Angel Dust

It was a cool Friday evening, the stars were out in full force, and I could smell the salty air emanating from the ocean. Traffic was light. It was the second night since I had passed my field training with Stofey. I was driving my patrol unit and felt confident. I was working alone. Oxnard was known as a place where people from Los Angeles—movie stars in many cases—came to purchase top-quality drugs. We had a marine port, which made it easy for drug smugglers to bring in their silent killer. I didn't know it yet, but this night was about to take a shocking turn.

I left the police station at about 9:35 p.m. in my black-and-white patrol car right after our squad meeting. I was watching a falling star while checking my unit in the parking lot, and I thought about how fortunate I was to have my job. I drove by Santa Clara Catholic Church, two blocks from the station, and as I passed in front of the church, I momentarily stopped to thank God for everything in my life. I asked him to protect me. My mood was buoyant. That morning I had spoken to a young college freshman about staying away from drugs, and he had listened to my advice about pursuing his education. I was a newlywed, and my wife was about to receive her CPA degree. I had also decided to start law school the following year as a part-time student at Pepperdine University in Malibu.

I was driving northbound on C Street. I came to a red light and stopped. I noticed a vehicle westbound on Gonzalez Road moving erratically. The driver noticed me while crossing the intersection. He attempted to hide his face by looking away from me. It was suspicious, to say the least. I waited for the green light, caught up to the vehicle, and followed it. I was about a block behind. The car swerved again about eighty yards in front of me. I thought that perhaps the young man had gotten nervous when he saw me following and had taken his eyes off the roadway. I continued following the vehicle and noticed that it zigzagged once more. The line had been crossed; it was time to stop the driver and check his condition. I was thinking about the best place to stop the vehicle and finally decided on a well-lit area on Ventura Road just past the following intersection. I reported the license plate to my dispatcher.

The driver made a right turn and continued northbound on Ventura Road. As I caught up to the vehicle, I turned on my red light, but the driver did not stop. Next I turned the siren on and off, and still received no response. This continued for about four or five blocks until the vehicle suddenly stopped. I called in my location, Holly Way and Ventura Road. The driver, a young white male who was about 5'8" and probably 140 pounds, got out of his vehicle and started walking toward me. I quickly got out of my unit and asked him to walk to the side of the roadway. He refused. As I approached him, I could not smell any alcohol on his breath, but his attitude was belligerent and strange. He would talk very politely and then suddenly become vociferous.

The longer we spent talking, the stranger his demeanor grew. He denied driving erratically. I asked him if he had taken any medication or had consumed any alcohol and he told me he hadn't, but I knew that I could not allow this person to continue driving. He was going to hurt somebody, or himself. I asked him for his car keys. I advised him to pick up the keys at the police station the following morning. I told him that I was going to have a taxi pick him up, and he said, "Okay."

When he was about to give me his car keys, he attempted to punch me in the face, and we began to struggle on the asphalt. We fought for what seemed like an eternity. As we were wrestling on the roadway, cars passed by, and I signaled at the drivers to stop. I yelled at them to help me. They just waited for us to get off the road, unwilling to get involved, before continuing on. Nobody helped. We continued struggling and hitting each other. We must have fought for about ten or fifteen minutes. I was getting very tired, and he was getting stronger and stronger. I was a well-built young man. I could bench press over 220 pounds in those days. But he became more aggressive, and I could not subdue him in spite of the wrestling and judo holds I attempted. To my shock and amazement, he picked me up effortlessly and threw me as though I were nothing more than a rag doll. He then punched me several times and knocked the wind out of me. I was running out of options.

Suddenly, he started going into convulsions. He could hardly breathe. I called for an ambulance several times. All of a sudden, he was unconscious. I made him as comfortable as I could on the asphalt and placed my jacket under his head. I asked the dispatcher to expedite an ambulance. Officer Stofey arrived to the scene first and asked me if I was okay. I could not believe what had happened. "It was only a routine stop," I told Stofey, "and look what happened." To be honest, though, there is no such thing as a routine stop. Stofey had instilled that lesson in me during my training. Anything is possible during a "routine" stop.

I placed the young man under arrest, although he was still unconscious. He was taken to Ventura County Hospital. I drove back to the police station to write my report, feeling bad for the suspect. Later that night, a detective who I will hereafter call Sergeant X came into the station and started interrogating me about the incident. He read me my Miranda rights. The sergeant interrogated me as though I were a criminal. It appeared to me that he wanted to catch me in a contradiction about what had happened during the arrest. I could not believe what was going on. "Here I am, attempting to serve and protect my community, and this guy is attempting to pin a crime on me," I thought.

The sergeant continued making subtle, derogatory comments. He insinuated that I had hurt the suspect and had been more aggressive than the situation warranted. Sergeant Lee Monahan, who was also in the office, listened, and after almost an hour, he interrupted. "Miguel told you what happened. What are you trying to do?"

Sergeant X was silent for a moment. He looked at me in a strange way. I could sense that he put no faith in my version of the events. He finally said, "Okay, that's all," and walked out of the detective's office.

Sergeant Monahan said to me, "Don't worry, son. You did your job properly. Go ahead and write your report."

Later that evening, Stofey came into the station to give me some encouragement. It took me the rest of the early morning to write the report. Between 6:00 and 7:00 a.m., the mother, a brother, and the father of the young man I had arrested came into the station. The watch commander called me from the squad room and told me they were waiting to see me. Stofey told me not to talk to them, but I felt that it was my responsibility to tell the young man's mother what had happened. I saw a middle-aged couple in front of me. Their faces were marked with sadness. I introduced myself and gave them an explanation. "I was protecting myself from his attacks," I told them. "I don't know why he acted the way he did."

"We understand, son. We knew that this was going to happen sooner or later," said the father. The mother said, "My son has been taking drugs for a while, and we knew that someday he was going to get into trouble." I felt miserable, my vision blurred with tears. They told me to take care of myself. The boy's father added, "We know how you feel, son; we know that you were doing your job. What happened to our son was because of drugs."

They gave me a handshake and walked out of the police station carrying their tragedy with them. I felt awful. After turning in my written report to the commanding officer at around 9:30 a.m., I went home.

The young man who assaulted me died in the hospital. I was living alone, and I cried most of that day. Chief Owens telephoned me and said to take some time off. I replied, "No, I want to go back on patrol." I was assigned to visit a psychologist, but I refused to see one. I spent all day thinking about the arrest. I thought about what I could have done differently to avoid what happened.

A day or two after the arrest, Officer Carlos Noriega picked me up at home and drove me to the Ventura County Coroner's office to talk with the coroner, who explained what caused the young's man death. "It was angel dust," he said. "It is a new drug to law enforcement. Not much is known about it in the country." I was one of the first officers in the country who had encountered a suspect with the drug in his system.

"That's why the suspect was getting stronger and stronger, as you stated in your report," explained the coroner. "This drug," he continued, "has many effects we do not know much about, especially when it's mixed with liquor, and the suspect had also consumed vodka or some type of liquor a few hours before you stopped him. You weren't responsible for his death," the coroner stated. He further explained that, "Angel dust and alcohol caused a cardiac arrest that could have happened at any time. Drugs do that to the system, and doctors never know when it can hit. With some people, drugs can give them a heart attack a few minutes after they take it. With others, it could take months or years. But drugs will get them sooner or later... The drug did it,"

Officer Noriega and I talked about what happened, and he tried to cheer me up, to reinvigorate me. Nothing he said reached me. He was concerned for my well-being, so he did not take me home, although I had asked him to. He did not want me to be alone. Carlos asked me if anybody was staying with me, and I responded, "No. My wife is away in school." He took me to the police station to see Chief Owens.

"You're a good man and a very conscientious police officer. What happened was not your fault," Chief Owens told me. He insisted that I should take a week or two off, and I told the chief that I would think about it.

Officer Noriega took me home, and that's where I stayed for a few days. I felt miserable. I cried. I questioned myself over and over as to what I could have done to prevent the incident. I finally came to the conclusion that I had done everything according to police procedure and had acted in accordance with my ethics. The death happened because the person had taken a potent, dangerous drug. Still, I was shaken. I contemplated leaving the department, but deep in my heart I knew that I had done my job properly and I wanted to continue doing it. I had arrested several drunk drivers previously and had witnessed nearly fatal accidents caused by intoxicated driving. My job was to prevent this from happening. I was well trained, and I wanted to continue doing everything possible to protect human dignity. I believed in our justice system. However, I thought I had hurt one of those citizens, and I'm only a rookie. How many more incidents like this will I have to face in the years to come? The question was constantly on my mind.

A police officer has an immense responsibility. At times I had to make life-or-death decisions instantaneously. "Orders to suspects were not obeyed,"

I thought on several occasions. The times were changing. Only the year before, people had obeyed when a police officer gave an order, and now there were more drugs in the street, and most of the arrests were drug related. This had a significant effect on people's behavior. Drugs, I observed, gave suspects a sense of power; and they were not going to make it easy for us as police officers. The same could be said for alcohol, but drunks were more docile than those under the influence of hard drugs. Quite often officers had to wrestle suspects down in order to arrest them. That was the law of the streets, and that was what I was going to be doing in the coming years if I wanted to remain on the force.

Crime indicators were increasing in the city of Oxnard, and I wanted to do my part to reverse them. We were experiencing a high index of robberies, assaults, burglaries, murders, bank robberies, and gang violence. To make matters worse, many individuals used to come to Oxnard from Los Angeles to purchase drugs like marijuana, heroin, coke, and crack. We had a serious crime element in the environment that was affecting our city, and many young people were involved, especially in drug-related crimes.

After much struggle, I renewed my commitment to police work. Five days later, I returned to my shift. Within the first two years of my law-enforcement career, I had investigated many crimes and had arrested countless suspects. I never stopped asking myself how human beings could be capable of perpetrating such dreadful acts against one another. I felt as though I had lived two lifetimes with all the cases I had handled, especially cases involving mothers who mistreated their own children, and drug related arrests. Those particular crimes dug deep into my soul and took root. You wouldn't believe the things I have seen: mothers who inflicted psychological and physical pain on their own children; repeat wife beaters; drug addicts; repeat child molesters and sex offenders; drunk drivers who acted without any consideration for other people's lives; rapists; murderers. I saw twelve-year-old children under the influence of glue or drugs. They sometimes had no idea where they were when I found them. Their minds were already becoming wasted. I was rapidly being initiated into a world of spiritual poverty and physical anguish that most people will not allow themselves to see.

The infractions had no respect for monetary or class divisions. I saw the wealthy purchasing drugs to get their kicks or to temporarily dissolve the emptiness at the core of their lives. I saw middle-and lower-class citizens stealing from their own families to purchase marijuana, cocaine, and heroin. Our society was becoming decadent in many respects, and our leaders were slowly making it worse by relaxing our laws and ethical norms. I felt helpless at times, swimming against this great, black tide, but felt it my duty to continue to protect the community I served to the best of my ability.

I grew frustrated as I watched the same offenders arrested over and over for the same crimes. I grew frustrated watching juveniles going in and out of juvenile hall for repeated offenses that earned them little more than a light slap on the hand by a judge. It seemed that at times, we were playing a cat-and-mouse game without thinking about how society as a whole was paying for the mistakes made by judges and legislators. These juveniles had more rights than the law-abiding citizens they offended against, or that's how it appeared to me as I bore witness to the fearsome cycles of recidivism.

Abused Children

I received a call at about 3:00 p.m. "Children crying" was the complaint received at the department. Officer Stofey also showed-up. When we arrived at the location, we found a two-year-old baby boy in his crib. He was crying in terrible hunger while trying to suck on an empty, dirty bottle. His five-year-old sister was trying to take care of him. The house was filthy. The little girl said, "My mommy went to the store. She'll be right back." As we spoke to this child, we noticed several cigarette burns on her thin, little arms. When I asked her how she got those marks, she responded, "My mommy puts her cigarette on my body when my baby brother cries." She pointed to her arms and showed us other burns on her shoulders. She smiled as she told us this. I think she was happy to have company.

Her baby face was covered with chocolate smudges, and her lovely brown eyes looked straight at us as we spoke to her. She had long, curly, light-brown hair. It was unkempt and partially covered her face: "I love my mommy very much. She burns me with her cigarettes because I don't take care of my baby brother. Mommy doesn't like my baby brother or me when we cry. I let him cry too much sometimes. We have to keep quiet when she goes away." As I listened to her comments during our conversation, I felt bad. I grabbed her little hand, and we walked to my patrol unit. She was the most beautiful little girl I had ever seen. Her face, with its warm smile, reminded me of Shirley Temple in the 1936 movie *Poor Little Rich Girl.*

"How can anyone treat a child this way?" I asked Stofey as we were leaving the house. "Well, partner," he said, "that's the real world. You're going to witness many things in this line of work that will make you sick to your stomach. You won't believe what people are capable of doing to their own kind." We took both children to the police station and surrendered them to Child Services. I learned that both were later adopted. Wherever they are, I hope they are well.

The Guest Who Came To Dinner

"Adam 3, station 3," said the dispatcher.

"Station 3, Adam 3," I responded.

"Adam 3. Contact Jennifer, a white haired lady on Fisher Drive. She will be meeting you outside her home regarding suspicious circumstances, possibly a theft. The suspect is in her home," indicated Nancy.

"Station 3. Adam 3, 10-4."

I responded to the call from my Beat 3, the downtown area. The incident was in Beat 6 by the beach. I was approximately 3 miles away and it took me about four minutes to arrive at the location.

Upon my arrival on Fisher Drive, a white haired woman was waiting for me on the sidewalk. She appeared to be nervous and was constantly looking toward her home, twenty yards away, as she was holding both of her hands together and compressing her fingers.

"Hello, Officer," she said in a quiet voice as I got out of my unit. "I am Jennifer; I called the police station. Thank you for coming so quickly." She extended her right arm to greet me. "Hi, Ma'am. How are you?" I responded, as we shook hands.

"Fine," she said. She seemed very nervous and worried as we started to speak.

"How may I help you, Ma'am? What seems to be the problem?" I asked.

"Well, I'm not sure how to say this officer, but I think that my friend, who my husband and I invited to dinner tonight, took my diamond ring," she said, as her voice started to break.

"Can you explain yourself, Ma'am," I said.

"Well, I am not sure officer. I had my yellow diamond wedding ring with me before my friend arrived. I was in my bedroom putting lotion on my hands, took off my ring and placed it inside the left top drawer of my bedroom dresser, and now it is gone," Jennifer said. "I cannot find my ring. I already looked in both drawers, and the ring is not there," she repeated. "Oh, my God, what am I going to do?" She took a deep breath, looked up at the full moon for a few seconds and said, "I am sorry, officer."

I felt bad and concerned for Jennifer. She wanted to cry. "If you placed your ring in the dresser drawer, Ma'am," I said, "it has to be there. Let's look for it carefully." As we were standing on the street, I was attempting to encourage Jennifer that she may have misplaced her ring. "Where was your husband when you placed your ring in the dresser?" I asked.

"He was next to me." She responded.

"Are you sure you placed your ring in the dresser? I asked, again.

"Yes, I am sure officer. I always put my ring there," Jennifer responded.

"Tell me, at what time did your guest arrive," I asked. "And what happened?"

"My husband and I are both retired and want to take a vacation, so we called our friend who works for the Social Security Administration," she said. "She arrived close to 8:30 p.m., and we talked for a while and had a few glasses of wine. We then had a nice dinner and spoke about our social security benefits."

"How long have you known her," I asked.

"Not too long. We met about a year an ago," she said.

"Is this the first time she visited your home," I asked.

"No," Jennifer responded. "She has been here several times before. I do not remember exactly how many, but maybe three or four times."

"Then what happened," I asked. "After you three had dinner?"

"Well, we had a glass of wine after dinner, and she asked if she could use the bathroom. I told her that the bathroom was next to my bedroom, and she walked to the back of the house. We have a small home," Jennifer continued. "After a few minutes had passed, my husband and I noticed that she was taking a long time in the bathroom, and my husband looked down the hallway and noticed both doors closed. My bedroom and the bathroom doors," she said. "I was washing the dishes and got worried that she was taking so long. I dried up my hands and went to my bedroom, and I noticed that my diamond ring was missing," Jennifer said. "I walked back to the living room and told my husband about the missing ring. We then waited for our friend to come out of the bathroom." Jennifer's eyes became watery and a couple of tears dropped from her eyes. She continued as she wiped her tears from her face with a small handkerchief.

"My friend came into the living room and unexpectedly said that she had to leave. I asked her to wait a few minutes, and I went to my bedroom to check again if my ring was in the dresser. My ring was not there. I then called the police right away from my bedroom."

I asked Jennifer where her friend was, and she responded, "Inside the house, speaking with my husband."

"May I see your bedroom and then speak with your husband," I asked Jennifer.

"Of course you may, officer," she said.

After walking into the four-room condominium, I greeted Jennifer's husband and their guest. The female guest who, was sitting on a yellow couch, responded very courteously and smiled at me. She was a beautiful woman, and I noticed that she appeared to have a wonderful personality as she carried on her conversation with Jennifer's husband. Jennifer took me to her bedroom, and I inspected the dresser. We then walked back to the living room.

"Good evening, Sir, Madam," I said. "May I speak with you, Sir?"

Jennifer's husband walked out with me and corroborated his wife's statements in detail. I proceeded into the house and asked Jennifer to show me her bedroom once more. I inspected the dresser and searched for the ring on the beautiful Persian rug covering the bedroom floor. I noticed that it was impossible to take any fingerprints from the dresser, as the wooden surface was porous.

After I continued questioning Jennifer and her husband in the living room, I noticed that their guest was getting nervous, and she was looking constantly at her watch. I asked Jennifer again if she was 100 percent certain that she had placed her ring in the dresser. "Yes, I did officer. I placed my diamond ring in my dresser's drawer right before my guest arrived," she responded. Her husband corroborated the statements, by adding, "Yes, officer. I saw my wife placing her diamond wedding ring in the dresser a few minutes before our guest arrived."

I looked at their guest and asked her politely if she had anything to say about the incident.

Looking very attentively straight into my eyes, she responded, "I have no idea what they are talking about. What are you insinuating officer? I did not take her ring." The guest then continued, to my surprise, in a somewhat angry, loud and authoritative tone of voice. "Do you have any idea who I am?"

"No, Ma'am," I responded, "and I don't think that it much matters as to who you are, Ma'am? I am investigating a theft." Suddenly, the guest lost her composure and yelled, "How dare you speak to me as though I am a thief; and to be making such an accusation! I am going to file a complaint against you." The lovely and happy face I had seen on the guest when I arrived had now turned into an angry expression. She suddenly stood up from the couch where she was sitting, gripped her beige color leather purse next to her, and walked out of the house. As the guest walked out, I followed her and told her that I wanted to speak with her. She became angry, approached me and slapped me on the left cheek. She was about to slap me again when I held her by the arm and placed her under arrest for battery on a police officer.

After handcuffing her and asking her several times to walk toward my police unit, she refused to do so. I asked her one last time to walk towards my police unit, and again, she refused. I then carried her on my shoulder to my unit and asked her to stand on her own feet as I was opening the back door behind the driver's side. The suspect yelled that I had hurt her back. She then pretended to have a bad back and indicated that she could not get into the unit. I asked her to sit down on the back seat and to slide in. The suspect spat in my face. She then kicked me in the groin with her right knee. I was in pain. I grabbed her by her head with my right hand, and forced her to sit down in my police unit. As she was setting down on the back seat, she leaned over on her back and kicked me with her right 3" heel on my chest, near my Adam's apple.

I could not believe her behavior. I was surprised! From that beautiful and charming lady she had been when I walked into the house, the subject had become a belligerent, rude and ugly person. She started yelling that I was going to be fired from my job because she knew people in high places. This lady was, indeed, full of surprises. Not only had she slapped me, spat on me, kneed me in the privates, and also attempted to stick her heel in my throat. I was very fortunate that she did not injure me; my bulletproof vest protected me from this lady's deadly heel. Once I got her into my police unit, I slammed the door and stood still for a while, leaning on my unit's trunk as I caught my breath. Jennifer walked over to see me and asked me if I was okay. She then brought me a glass of water.

After a couple of minutes, I radioed the dispatcher.
"Station 3, Adam 3,"

"Adam 3, Station 3," Nancy responded.

"I have a suspect in custody. Advise the Watch Commander to have someone available to conduct a body search on a female," I said.

"10-4," she responded.

While driving back to the police station, I was thinking about how close this lady had come to seriously hurting me. I was thinking of how this call could have turned into a serious injury incident; or how I possibly could have ended up dead if the suspect's shoe heel would have penetrated my throat. I was upset at myself because I had underestimated the suspect. I still had a lot to learn about people's behavior.

Upon my arrival to the station, the subject was searched by one of our female dispatchers, and nothing was found on her. However, when the booking officer checked the suspect's purse and took inventory of her property, there was a yellow stone ring inside the purse that matched the description Jennifer had given me of her 3.5 Carat yellow diamond ring.

I read the suspect her Miranda's Rights and she refused to speak with me. I filed grand theft charges against the suspect as well as battery on a police officer. She was booked.

At approximately 12 a.m., I called Jennifer to advise her about her guest having the diamond ring. She asked me if she could pick-up her ring and I instructed her to call the district attorney's office to retrieve her property, as it was going to be held as evidence. Jennifer was very happy that her ring had been recovered.

"Interesting," Jennifer said, as we were about to finish our conversation, "how a good friend could become your worst enemy."

Several weeks later, I received a post card saying, "Thank your for getting my ring back; it means a lot to me. We are celebrating our 50th wedding anniversary."

Jennifer and her husband were in Puerto Vallarta, enjoying their love affair.

YOUR ACTIONS CAN SHATTER THE LIVES OF OTHER PEOPLE AND FORCE THEM TO PAY A PORTION OR ALL OF THE CONSEQUENCES.

The Hells Angels

RESPECT BEGETS RESPECT, HATE BEGETS HATE, AND LOVE BEGETS LOVE.

I was assigned to Beat 4 that summer evening and had just finished patrolling the industrial area between Pacific Coast Highway (State Route 1) and Channel Islands Boulevard. It was approximately 2:00 a.m. I always wore special white thermal pajamas underneath my uniform when assigned to the morning shift, and I was sweating. It usually got cold during the early-morning hours in our town due to the ocean mist. I did not like my police jacket. It was bulky and made me look like a little stuffed bear. I was not agile when I wore it, and I wanted to keep loose in case the job demanded it. I also hated turning on my patrol unit's heater. I would get a stuffy nose whenever I had the heater on for more than a few minutes, and having to walk into the cool air after being in the heat did not help my body temperature. Oxnard's constant weather changes during the early-morning hours—beautiful weather would quickly turn into a thick cold blanket of fog.

I parked my police unit next to a gas station on Pacific Coast Highway south of Date Street, close to a row of eucalyptus trees, and began to write a traffic collision report. I could not finish it earlier as I had several calls since starting my shift at 9 p.m. I was behind by three reports: residential burglary; a drunk I had arrested who was causing a disturbance in a hotel; and a commercial burglary report, which was the first call, to which I was dispatched that evening. I wanted to go home after finishing my shift at 7 a.m. My wife and I had planned to go to the theater in Los Angeles that day. We wanted to see Yul Brynner in *The King and I*. We had planned to spend all day in L.A., so I was going to drive to the St. Bonaventure Hotel in downtown, take a long nap, and then see the musical that evening. We were going to spend my three days off visiting the J. Paul Getty Museum in Santa Monica which had brought in a new art exhibition, and do research at UCLA for my wife's thesis. I was excited to see Yul Brynner again. He was my favorite actor. I had seen him in the same play four years earlier in the spring of 1973 when I was a sophomore in college.

I had taken my unfinished report out of my briefcase, placed it on the passenger seat, and began to go over my notes and organize my thoughts. I was half way through my report when I noticed two guys fighting outside a business west of where I was parked, about eighty yards away. I hurriedly threw all my papers in my briefcase, closed it, and drove to where the subjects were fighting. The subjects stopped fighting as they saw my patrol unit approaching. I radioed my location and the incident to the radio dispatcher. I exited my patrol unit and called out to the two men, "What's going on?"

"Nothing officer," replied a burly man, 6'1" and about 200 pounds. We just had a disagreement in the bar and we walked out to resolve our problem. But we are okay now. I don't want to spend tonight in jail."

"Good," I said, "I would hate to take you guys in over a misunderstanding."

"No, Sir, we are just settling our differences, but we are okay," the other man responded. "We don't want any problems with the law. We just came here to have a good time with our girls and I got a bit jealous. But everything is okay," he said.

"Okay guys, I hope you're both going to be fine. I would hate to return and take you in," I said, and left the area.

I returned to the parking lot where I had parked prior to the incident and continued writing my report.

As I finished writing a different report, I notice six motorcyclists traveling at a high rate of speed westbound on Pacific Highway. Four of the motorcyclists made the yellow light at the intersection; the light turned red, and the last two subjects went through the red light.

I radioed the Beat 2 officer and advised him about the traffic violation by the two motorcyclists. He was busy on a call. I then proceeded to follow the bikers. I caught up to them about a mile from the location of the traffic violation, turned on my unit's red and blue lights and pulled them over.

"Station 3, Adam 4, Oxnard Boulevard and Third Street, underneath the overpass, two blocks away from our police station. Two motorcyclists." I had noticed that the subjects were Hells Angels. As I got out of my police unit, my body suddenly felt cold; I felt a shiver run down my spine. I hesitated for a few seconds and decided to approach them cautiously. "Good morning," I said to the motorcyclists. "May I please have both of your drivers' licenses?"

As I approached one of the subjects, he stood up from his motorcycle seat, and I noticed his enormous body as he received his partner's driver's license and then gave both documents to me. They turned off their roaring motorcycle engines.

I responded, "Thank you, sir." I continued with a firm voice, "Do you both know why I stopped you?" Both of the subjects got off their motorcycles, and I asked them to walk to the sidewalk. Several cars drove by northbound Oxnard Blvd., and I did not want them to get hit by a passing motorist. As they walked closer to me, one of the motorcyclists, a man about 6'3" and roughly 230 pounds, with muscles over his muscles in his arms, said in a soft voice, "Yes, sir. We ran the red light back there. We did not see any cars, so we just continued, not stopping for the red light. We made a mistake, officer. We were attempting to catch up with our buddies. We have been riding for several hours from San Diego, and we still have a long way to go. We are heading to Oakland."

Many negative thoughts came to my mind. They were, after all, Hells Angels! How the hell am I going to handle this situation? These guys are rough and have no respect for the law. I looked north and south on Oxnard Blvd, hoping that another officer would back me up quickly. I did not see anyone in sight. I remembered how the Hells Angels were said to be cop killers in the 60s, and many other thoughts continued popping into my brain. I was recollecting many negative stories I had read while in college, and other stories I had heard from fellow officers.

I have to calm down, I told myself. I must do what I have to do, and finish with this situation as quickly as possible. I had no choice. I had stopped these guys for running a red light, and now it was time to face my responsibility and handle the situation properly. Negative thoughts continued to invade my mind and I felt somewhat afraid. I kept on looking at the other four bikers returning to where I had stopped their friends. By this time, the other four members of the group had made a U-turn and parked about 30 yards north of us on Oxnard Boulevard. They were all dressed in Levis, with silver color chain adornments protruding from their clothing, dark sun glasses, and wearing German-style motorcycle helmets. They all had the distinct "Hells Angels" insignia patch on the back of their sleeveless Levi jackets.

I asked the subjects several questions, and they were very courteous in their responses. Their answers were quick and to the point. Not a word more, not a word less. Our conversation lasted for about five minutes, the first minute of which felt like time had stopped. However, as time passed, they were apologetic and sincere in their responses as to why they had run the red light. After I had the dispatcher check their names for warrants--and the inquiries returned clear--I gave them a warning and returned their licenses.

"Thank you sir," I said to each of the motorcyclists, "for being so cooperative."

"It is our pleasure to be treated with respect. Thank you, Sir," the tallest of the subjects responded. The other subject just looked at me with an expression of disbelief. He then winked and said, "Have an excellent day officer. It was nice meeting you." They got on their motorcycles, started their motorcycles, revving engines, saluted me, and rode away with the group ahead. I stared at them, myself in disbelief. They all waved good-bye at the precise moment that two two-man patrol units arrived, and I felt relieved and my heartbeat slowed down.

For the first time in my young life as a rookie cop, I experienced an indescribable fear. But I forced myself to be in command of the situation when I found myself alone with these bikers. However, after I had exchanged a few words with the subjects, I learned that they were respectful and not at all what society perceived them to be. At least not in this case. I was brought up to always treat people with respect, regardless of their social status; and these two bikers I had stopped – presumed trouble because they were Hells Angels -- were gentlemen. But most importantly, I learned a lesson that night about people with whom we are not accustomed to dealing: Respect begets respect, regardless of a person's "label" by society.

Arresting a Chief

When you are in doubt, be still, and wait; when doubt no longer exists for you, then go forward with courage. So long as mists envelope you, be still; be still until the sunlight pours through and dispels the mists—as it surely will. Then act with courage.

Chief White Eagle

At around 5 a.m., I made a right turn west bound on 5th Street off Rose Ave. When I was about to make a left turn onto Commerce Drive, I noticed an oncoming black 1956 Chevy pick-up truck going east bound on 5th St, zigzagging at a slow rate of speed with no headlights on. I turned on my overhead red and blue lights and yelled at the driver to stop. I made a quick U-turn and followed the vehicle for about fifty yards. The vehicle was stopped in the middle of the street. The driver got out of his vehicle and attempted to walk toward my unit, leaving the door open. I rapidly got out of my patrol unit and hurried to meet him in an attempt to get him off the roadway. He was a huge man, at least 6'3", and over 250 pounds. As soon as I saw him, he reminded me of a wrestler. In fact, I thought he was a Samoan wrestler I saw a couple of times at wrestling matches in L.A. in the late 60s when I was a teenager growing up in Oxnard. He certainly appeared to be identical to that well-known gladiator. I was excited to see him, as I had seen many famous movie and sports stars in town having dinner at different restaurants in the area.

When I reached the subject, there was a strong odor of alcohol on his breath. His clothing was disheveled, and his balance was unstable. He indicated that he was going to park the vehicle properly, and as he attempted to get back into the driver's side of his pick-up truck, he almost fell head first and held on to the steering wheel. I said, "Sir, I am sorry, but you cannot get into your car."

"Of course I can," he said, and again, he attempted to get into his vehicle and stumbled for a second time.

"Sir," I yelled, "you will not get in that car!"

"Yes, I can. There is nothing wrong with me. You can give me a test if you want, and I will pass it. I am not drunk," he said. "Look, I can stand on my right foot alone without any problems." As he attempted to do so, he almost fell. He then attempted to start a Native American ceremonial dance and began chanting.

"Sir, I need you to give me your car keys," I said in a loud tone of voice. "You are not driving anywhere." He stopped his dancing and in a slurred speech, he indicated that he was going to recite the alphabet to show me that he was not drunk.

"I am okay," he said. "I just have a few more miles to go. I am heading to Santa Barbara." He was driving the opposite direction. I asked him to perform a final test – "walk an imaginary straight line." He agreed to do so, but he could not maintain his balance. When he attempted to perform the test, I held on to him and we both almost fell backward.

"I am sorry to tell you sir, but you are not going anywhere as you cannot drive your vehicle. You are under arrest," I said. "Please turn around so I can handcuff you."

"Okay, I give up," he said cheerfully and apologetically. "You got me, officer. But I can assure you that I am okay." As we were walking to my police unit, I had to help him maintain his balance.

Six or seven months later, I was subpoenaed to testify in this case. As I gave my testimony of the arrest, the defense attorney was playing with words, alluding to my inexperience with drugs as a rookie police officer. The defense attorney attempted to use my testimony against me, claiming that I had no idea of how a medicated person would act versus a person under the influence of alcohol or drugs. He was wrong. I petitioned the judge, indicating that I could not give yes and no answers as the defense attorney was asking. Each question he asked me needed an explanation. Not helping this matter was the fact that the young deputy district attorney who was handling the case was not making any objections to the defense's line of questioning--at least that's how I felt. He allowed the defense attorney to cross-examine me as he pleased. I had to refer to my report several times for information due to the length of time it took to bring this case to the court, and I needed to refresh my memory regarding some of the details.

I never found out what the verdict was in this case, but I remember how the defense attorney argued that the man I had arrested was the chief of an important American Indian tribe in Northern California and that his behavior was always proper; the defendant was affluent in his community and a law-abiding citizen. He was a virtuous man, argued his attorney, so the Judge should give a not-guilty verdict.

Undercover: The Chase

It was around 10:30 p.m. I was working undercover in a bar in the area of Hueneme Road and J Street. I was witnessing a drug deal in progress when a security guard approached me and asked for my identification card. I explained to him that I was twenty-six and that I was waiting for a couple of friends. He continued to ask for my ID. When I failed to show it, he started to push me around. I pretended to be drunk. I was dressed in light blue Levis, a white T-shirt, and a torn brown leather jacket. He grabbed me and forced me up against the wall, and I knocked him down.

The suspects looked toward us and exited the bar through the back door, which led into the alley. As I started to run out of the bar, I ran into two ladies who were coming out of the bathroom. I called out an apology as I ran out of the building. I could not see any movement in the back parking lot. I started to look for the two suspects, but I couldn't hear anything nor see a car moving. As I kept searching, I transmitted into a mike, hidden under my shirt, to my partners, "I'm in the back parking lot of the bar. Back me up."

I saw someone about forty yards away walking in the alley. He fit the description of one of the suspects I had observed in the bar. "I'm following a suspect in the alley northbound," I said to my partners as I broke into a run. I followed the suspect for two blocks. He hurried up a stairway in one of the apartment complexes about sixty yards ahead of me. Unexpectedly, I saw three ladies in the alley approaching me. They stopped a few feet behind me. One of them, the leader I presumed, walked toward me and asked my name. I casually gave it to her. "You owe us ten bucks," she said. "You spilled our drinks and we want our money now." I told her that I had no idea what she was talking about.

"Well, if you have some twenty-dollar bills, you can have some fun with us in our room," she said.

"No thank you," I said to her. I started to walk away from them toward the apartment complex. She got upset and pushed me, and the other girls tried to hit me with their purses. I told them that I was busy looking for a friend, and one of them responded, "I'm your friend. I'm your mama. You don't need to look for me anymore. Let's you and I have some fun."

I didn't want to blow my cover. I ignored the pushing and made a few comments to them. They chased me in the alley for about twenty yards. I admit to being a little impressed that they were surprisingly fast. I continued speaking into the mike, thinking that my partners would arrive at any moment, but my transmission was in vain. I finally lost the ladies, but I also lost my suspect. I did not see which apartment he had entered. There were several buildings, each with six apartments.

About ten minutes later, I saw my partners running in the alley toward me. Detective Dellinger, a bit out of breath, asked, "Where were you, partner? We've been looking for you."

"Are you okay partner," asked detective Gomez.

"Hell, where was I?" I responded. "Three prostitutes chased me. What happened to you guys? I was giving you instructions to follow me into the alley."

"We couldn't hear you. All we heard was the security guard arguing with you, a hell of a lot of music, and a lot of jumbled words. A few minutes later, we heard the words 'in the alley.'" Dellinger responded.

"This has turned out to be a hell of an undercover operation, hasn't it?" I said. "I saw the deal go down, but I lost the suspects. We don't have anything!"

As we walked back to our undercover van through the bar, the security guard apologized. I responded, "Forget it. It's okay, but remember me next time."

"How could I know you were a cop? You look like an eighteen-year-old high school kid!" He replied.

I turned to my partners. "It looks like my first assignment as a detective was a Mickey Mouse operation. Let's try again another day."

"You can't win 'em all. We'll get the dealers next time," Detective Gomez said.

Boys with Guns

It was about 10:30 p.m. when I received the call.

"Loud music on Fournier Street south of Channel Islands Boulevard." As I drove onto Fournier Street I noticed a young man standing in the middle of the street about one hundred yards in front of me. I quickly turned my headlights off and parked my police unit about eighty yards away from him. I walked slowly up the sidewalk, hiding behind vehicles. The young man walked to the east side of the street and leaned into a vehicle. He was speaking to someone; I was too far to hear what he said. He walked to the front yard of a home and started urinating on the lawn. I asked for backup and heard an Oxnard officer say, "Four Boy, will back up." I also heard a Port Hueneme officer say, "Copied; will back up."

A Ventura County sheriff's deputy responded, "Will be there in two." I ran toward the suspects' vehicle, continuing to hide behind the parked cars. When I arrived at the suspect's car, I found two teenagers passed out in the back seat. The windows were down, and there was a very strong odor of alcohol. Each of them was holding onto a rifle. I ran toward the subject who was urinating and told him not to make any noise. I ordered him to slowly turn around and face me. The young man was reaching for his waist grabbed his hand from behind and at the same time felt a small-caliber revolver tucked in his front waistband. He was about to pull the weapon when I knocked him to the ground, took the revolver out of his hand, and handcuffed him with his arms behind his back. I left him face down on the front lawn and whispered in his ear, "Don't move or say a damn thing." I then ran back to the parked vehicle where the other two subjects were passed out. As I was approaching the car, the arrested subject yelled, "Watch out! There's a cop!" One of the youths began to stir.

I took my weapon out of my holster and yelled, "Don't grab the rifle!" I quickly opened the back passenger door of the vehicle. The young man near me attempted to grab his rifle, and I hit him in the face with my weapon as I pulled the rifle out of the car by the barrel. He yelled, "Wake up, man! A pig!" I took the second rifle as well. The youth who had held it was still passed out. As the last kid came to, he mumbled, "Shit, a pig!" The effects of the alcohol helped make my job easier. I was relieved. I never again wanted to experience what I had gone through as a rookie. The first incident was never far from my mind.

Meanwhile, the deputy sheriff had arrived at the scene and within a few seconds, the Port Hueneme officer was also helping me handcuff the suspects. I thanked God for helping me resolve the situation as painlessly as possible.

When Officer Don Lanning, one of my partners, arrived, he checked the vehicle and saw several rifles in the trunk. I had the vehicle impounded and taken to the police station to be searched. Several other weapons were found and tagged as evidence. Later that night when I was checking the serial number of the weapons, I found that all the rifles had been taken during a burglary at Kmart, a call Officer Stofey and I had investigated six weeks earlier. All three suspects were arrested.

I later found out the suspects had received minor juvenile hall sentences. Our court system was a joke, a belief shared by many of my fellow officers. We were arresting juveniles, most of who were repeat offenders, and they were only being sentenced lightly for their crimes before being allowed to return to their communities.

An Influential Young Man

At approximately 11:00 p.m., I followed a luxurious, sporty vehicle making a right turn southbound on Victoria Avenue off Hemlock Street. The vehicle zigzagged several times. As I made the stop, a young driver got out of the car and walked toward my patrol unit. I hurried out of the unit and asked him to step on the sidewalk. He did. As I approached him, I noticed that he could not maintain his balance properly, and his speech slurred when he spoke. After a few minutes, I arrested him. When I handcuffed him, he offered me money to let him go. He indicated that he lived across the street and that he had a great deal of cash at home. "I live there, in Mandalay Bay," he said. It was an expensive home area near the beach with a yacht entrance for each home.

"If you let me go, I'll give you anything you want."

I transported the suspect to the police station. While he was being fingerprinted, he told me that he also owned homes in New York and Rio de Janeiro. He asked me, "How much do you make?" The suspect was bragging as to how much money he made in a few weeks versus what I made in a year and made several jokes about how long it would take me to make what he made in a month. The subject continued speaking as to how he was going to leave town and not show up in court. He then stated, "I will get out before you ever finish your police report. I know people."

I asked the watch commander to have a judge sign a petition to hold the suspect in custody until his court date, which was done. However, the twenty-three-year-old blond-haired man was walking out of the police station before I had finished writing my report. I remember how I felt--I was angry! I had arrested this young man with a couple of charges, including offering a bribe to police officer, and he was walking out. The young man waved good-bye with a big smile on his face as he winked when he passed in front of me. He knocked on the window so I would see him leave the police station. When I asked the lieutenant why the suspect was released, his response was just a shrug of his shoulder indicating that he didn't know. I could not believe his response. I did not say anything and continued with my report. I was upset, more so because this lieutenant had told me that a judge had indicated that this suspect was not going to be released on bail. I was never subpoenaed to this case, either.

Arresting a Friend

I was checking the bathrooms at Colonia Park when I found a young man in dirty clothes passed out. He was drugged, leaning on a corner wall. He smelled like a corpse that had somehow managed to crawl out of its grave. When I woke him, he stared at me for a while as though he could not quite believe I existed. I checked his eyes, tongue, and both hands. I discovered a fresh needle mark on his left arm. In addition there were needle tracks, old ones, dotting both of his arms and the spaces between his toes. I then noticed that he looked surprisingly familiar. When he became more aware of what was going on, he said, "Is that you, Miguel?"

"Yes," I responded. "You're Paul, aren't you?" Oh God, I thought. Paul had been one of my best friends in high school. I had not seen him since 1971 when we graduated from high school. He had been a handsome young man with a bright future when we parted ways after graduation. And now here he was, six years later in 1977. I helped him stand up.

"Is it sad to see me like this?" he asked.

"Of course it is. Why, Paul? What's wrong with you? How can you put this crap in your body? What the hell is wrong with you?"

I arrested him and transported him to the police station. After having a long talk with him, I placed him in jail and told him that I did not want to see him like that ever again. He was booked. I got Paul medical help and wished him well on his recovery. We drifted out of touch again.

In 1984, I walked into a business in Oxnard, and Paul was standing behind the front counter waiting on customers. As soon as he saw me, he said, "Sir, it's good to see you! Are you okay? I heard that you were injured." He had his own business and he looked well, but he had clearly aged beyond his years. Paul yelled out a name and a small child emerged from the back storage room. He introduced me to his boy, about five or six years old, and thanked me for getting him off drugs. "Son, I want you to meet this man. I owe him my life. He got me off drugs, and that's why daddy is here with you."

It was rare moments like this that made me feel the value of my work. As tempting as cynicism might be, I find it contradicted by the extraordinary capacity that human beings possess to make real, lasting changes in their lives regardless of how far they might have fallen.

Kids, Just Playing

It was around 1:00 a.m. and I was heading to the city garage to fill my unit with gas. I was almost out. I noticed a vehicle with four subjects in it and the vehicle did not have a license plate. Looking closer, I saw that the subjects in the back seat had what appeared to be rifles. I had to make a decision to follow them or get gasoline. I called for backup and continued following the vehicle. I knew that I could run out of gas at any moment, but I did not want to let these subjects get away. I followed them for about three minutes and noticed that one subject had ducked down in the back seat.

Finally, I noticed a unit driving northbound on Saviers Road, as I was southbound approaching Five Points. My partner made a U-turn when he reached the intersection and was now behind me. We switched over to another band, and I relayed all my information to my arriving partner. I could see in my rearview mirror two other units approaching us from behind, as they simultaneously radioed, "3A, 2A, behind you." My Beat 5 partner and I were thinking through our strategy as to how we were going to make the stop when suddenly I ran out of gas. All the units passed me to back up the Beat 5 unit. A few minutes later, the shift sergeant arrived and was upset with me. It was as though I had committed a mortal sin, and it felt harsh; but he was right. Nevertheless, I had been forced to make a decision, and I thought it best to follow the vehicle.

When my partners cleared the call, I was informed that the supposed guns I had seen turned out to be broomsticks painted black. The subject who ducked his head down was just playing around; that's what they told the officers. Four juveniles had played a bad joke on me. They had all been in juvenile hall several times. They had learned how far they could go with their games while still being protected by the law. This particular game cost over forty-five minutes of four police officers' time.

Our Code

I am proud to say that members of the Oxnard Police Department were very strict as far as ethics were concerned. There was no corruption, and if an officer was found guilty of an ethics violation, the penalty was severe. Our policy was very specific. We had to pay for everything, and I do mean everything. We were not even allowed to accept free cup of coffee, much less any type of gift. For example, we had an officer who was discovered favoring a prostitute and accepting special favors from her. When this was discovered, the officer received the worst penalty any officer can get — he was fired immediately. He lost his honor and his family.

We all believed in our code of ethics and followed it to the letter. Police officers transferring to our department from out of state were not accepted without receiving our training. None of us were ever under orders or pressured to reach a specific quota of moving violations or arrests. We patrolled our assigned beats at our own discretion and used our own judgment to determine what sections of our beats we would patrol. Our only objective was to decrease crime.

As for our off-duty behavior, we were respectful and professional, and we served as an example to our community. People certainly make mistakes on occasions, but those who broke the code, whether on or off duty, were never able to escape severe consequences. We were Oxnard's finest and strongly believed in the Law Enforcement Code of Ethics, our oath as members of the Peace Officers' Association for the State of California:

Law Enforcement Code of Ethics.

As a Law Enforcement Officer, my fundamental duty is to serve mankind; to safeguard lives and property; to protect the innocent against deception, the weak against oppression or intimidation, and the peaceful against violence or disorder; and to respect the constitutional rights of all men and women to liberty, equality and justice.

I will keep my private life unsullied as an example to all; maintain courageous calm in the face of danger, scorn, or ridicule; develop self-restraint; and be constantly mindful of the welfare of others. I will be honest in thought and deed in both my personal and official life. I will be exemplary in obeying the laws of the land and the regulations of my department. Whatever I see or hear of a confidential nature or that is confided to me in my official capacity will be kept ever secret unless revelation is necessary in the performance of my duty.

I will never act officiously or permit personal feelings, prejudices, animosities, or friendships to influence my decisions. With no compromise to crime and with relentless prosecution of criminals, I will enforce the law courteously and appropriately without fear or favor, malice or ill will, never employing unnecessary force or violence and never accepting gratuities.

I recognize the badge of my office as a symbol of public faith, and I accept it as a public trust to be held so long as I am true to the ethics of police service. I will constantly strive to achieve these objectives and ideals, dedicating myself before God to my chosen profession... law enforcement.

Child Molestation

I was assigned to Beat 6, the beach area, when I was called in to the police station at about 3:00 p.m. to take a report on a possible child sex offense. When I arrived and spoke with the mother, I discovered that the victim was a four-year-old child. I told the little girl about my niece "Annie" and how she reminded me of her. We spoke about her favorite cartoons and toys and about her mommy. We became friends. As I asked her about her father, she became upset. My heart broke as I heard what her stepfather had done to her. He had molested the innocent little girl several times.

"It hurts a lot," she said, "when he plays with me." As I listened to her story and spoke to the mother, I wanted to go out to the oil platform in the Santa Barbara Channel Islands and arrest that bastard immediately. Her step-father worked on the oil platforms and would come ashore once or twice a month, and that's when he sexually abused the child. I finished the report and submitted it. I was beyond upset; I was disgusted with the whole façade of humanity. I remember calling the detective in charge of crimes against children and asking him to proceed on this case as quickly as possible. I had taken a few of these reports previously, and they never failed tear me up inside. I rarely had the heart to do this type of follow-up when I was assigned to them. I took these cases too personally. Child sex offenders were especially repulsive to me.

I had spoken to a couple of judges as to why some child molesters had only been sentenced to a few years in jail when they should have received longer jail terms. The response I received was, "It's complicated." What about the child? What about the child's life? What about the trauma the family experiences? What about the victims? "Complicated", I thought. How could I tell a mother that the sex offender who committed the crime on her child was a repeat offender out on parole? Sex offenders should be thrown in jail for life, I thought. My belief was that judges were too lenient on sexual offences perpetrated against children and women. Punishments had to be harsher if they were to serve as an effective deterrent against repeat offenders.

After I left law enforcement, a three-strike law was enacted in California. I believe this helped matters a bit, but did it? I read in the Los Angeles newspaper that a person who had committed a crime—his third strike, so I read—was sentenced to life in prison because he stole a pack of cigarettes. Now it had been taken too far. Will we ever have a sound system of justice based on common sense?

Community Service

During my three days off, I would speak with young people and parents. I visited them at their homes, at a park, or at neighborhood meetings. I did not take every young teenager I arrested due to a minor drug offense to jail. Often I would call in the parents to the police station and speak to them. Many of these young men stayed away from drugs and continued going to school after I spoke with them. I attempted to keep close contact with them, as all I wanted was to convince them that drugs were not the answer to their problems or any way to live their lives. "Drugs will only burn out your brains. Is that what you want?" I would ask them.

Our drug problems were increasing dramatically in the late 1970s in Oxnard and throughout the county. At the same time, there were outstanding warrants issued for many citizens, including otherwise law-abiding citizens in Ventura County, for simple traffic violations. Taking everyone to jail was not going to solve our problems. This need to find a fair means of redress acted upon as an impetus in my decision to become involved with the community during my days off. Better relationships between the police department and the people they serve are vital if we want to bring peace into our communities.

The KKK Comes To Town

It was a hot summer day when the Ku Klux Klan's Grand Dragon and his followers came to Oxnard. I was astonished when Lieutenant Hawkins gave me my assignment; I couldn't believe it. I was assigned to protect the Grand Dragon at his hotel, The Wagon Wheel Junction. I asked incredulously, "That's my beat assignment?"

I yelled across the squad meeting room, "Lieutenant Hawkins!"

"Yes, Officer Pinzón," he said.

"With all due respect, Sir, how can I protect someone who hates Black Americans, immigrants, like me? Do you really expect me to protect those men, men who don't agree with my values or respect my human dignity? How can I protect a group that breaks the law?" I have rarely been so upset in my life. I recalled that unpleasant moment in college when a professor had stated in class that "Mexicans should go back to where they came from." I hadn't said a damn thing at that time. This time was going to be different. I was going to defend my beliefs, my dignity and my rights.

I told the watch commander that he might as well put another officer to watch me because I might break the law and do to the KKK what they had done to so many Black American families in the past. And furthermore, "I might arrest the SOB Grand Dragon myself and a few of his people. I'll find a probable cause."

There was complete silence in the squad room. No one said anything. Lieutenant Hawkins pretended that I had not said anything and rearranged the assigned beats. A white officer was assigned to protect the Klan group in Beat 1, and I was reassigned to the farthest beat from that area, Beat 6, by the beach. No one liked Beat 6. Nothing happened there except for surfers drinking in public, an occasional burglary, or a smashed window. Lieutenant Hawkins never said anything to me about the incident; neither did any of the other top brass or officers--they all knew exactly how I felt about racism.

Back From the Dead

Officer Mike Alford and a young rookie officer he was training received a call at about 11:00 p.m. in the downtown area; Beat 2, Bonita and Sixth Street. A young man in a suit was stumbling in the street. I quickly backed up the officer and noticed when I arrived that he was holding a man by the arm as he was questioning him. I approached them and almost recoiled at the strong odor of alcohol coming from the man's body. As Alford let him go, the man stumbled and almost fell, and we grabbed him.

As we asked him questions, he responded that he had been taking medication. I noted his answer and was about to ask another question when the man suddenly underwent a severe seizure and urinated in his pants. We laid him on the sidewalk while his convulsions increased in intensity. Alford quickly asked the dispatcher to expedite an ambulance to our location.

The young man became immobile, and his heart stopped. We revived him by performing CPR. As he came to, he vomited on both of us. A few minutes passed, and his heart stopped again. I quickly cleaned the vomit from his mouth with my handkerchief and repeated the CPR procedure. We revived him again. The ambulance finally arrived and took him to the hospital. When we cleared the call, we returned to the police station to get cleaned up and returned to our respective beats.

Later that night Mike told me that the twenty-five-year-old man was okay. Officer Alford and I spoke about the incident a couple of days later, and we both felt proud we had saved a life. There are few things as satisfying in this world. The following week the young man's wife called the police station and spoke to the watch commander, Lieutenant Hawkins. He told me about the call. She had called to thank us. Alford's proper CPR procedures had saved the man's life; I just assisted him and followed his instructions. Officer Alford was one of the finest partners I had during my time on the force.

Gladys

One night Lieutenant Hawkins sent me to see if someone named Gladys was all right. It was about 11:30 p.m. when the dispatcher said, "Charles 4, see the lady at the 300 block of Channel Islands."

"10-4," I responded.

When I arrived I saw a lady who was probably in her late seventies standing in the middle of the street waiting for me, directing traffic. I realized that she was what we call a 51-50 (someone suspected of being mentally unstable). She was a little out of this world but sane enough to hold a conversation, and take care of her. I approached Gladys and persuaded her to walk with me on the sidewalk. She told me that she lived in the house facing us, so I walked her in. I entered the house, never suspecting what awaited me inside.

I had never seen so many cats in one place as I did in her living room. The smell was indescribable. I almost vomited. I asked her if she wouldn't mind continuing our conversation outside. I couldn't take another second in that place. I stood on the front lawn of Gladys' house, wondering if this was all some sort of bad joke, when Officer Stofey arrived and said, "Hi, Gladys, how are you? You haven't called the station in a while. I thought you'd moved out of town." Gladys had followed me outside.

"You know that I can't do that," she replied. "Who will take care of my kittens? I'm fine, thank you for asking, Officer Stofey. You're still as good looking as always."

"I just dropped by to check on my partner and see if he was taking good care of you. I want to introduce him to you. This is Officer Pinzón, and he'll be taking care of you from this day forward. So whenever you have a problem, just call the station and ask for him."

"Thank you." She inspected me carefully. "I like him," she said. "He looks too young, but he seems to know his job well. I bet you trained him, didn't you?"

"Gladys, you're too sweet," said Stofey.

I walked Gladys back to her home. It took me about fifteen minutes to persuade her to stay home and say good-bye. In that time she gave me the names of about fifteen cats, not a single one of which I now remember. She kept on wanting to go out and direct traffic until I convinced her it was a bad idea.

When I saw Stofey later during our shift, he was laughing.

"Hi partner, so you finally met Gladys!" he said.

Every senior officer knew Gladys except me, even though I had been at the department for two years. Gladys had been calling the department since the early 1960s whenever she felt lonely. After our introduction, she would call the station occasionally and ask for me. I was sent to see her two or three other times. One day, she just stopped calling.

I passed by her home numerous times and noticed that a different family had moved in. I never found out what happened to Gladys. As police officers, people come in and out of our lives and we cannot help but wonder and care about them; I wondered what had happened to all the cats, too. Gladys wanted me to take care of them and had named one after me. "Miguelito," she called it.

Irresponsible Cop, No Backup

It was about around 12:00 a.m. when I heard a call being transmitted to the officer in *La Colonia*, Beat 2. "Burglary in progress. Man seen on the roof of a drug store on Cooper Road," stated the dispatcher.

"10-4," responded the mid-shift officer.

I hurried to the area from Beat 1. I was about four miles from the location given by the dispatcher and said, "Adam 1, will back up."

"10-4," acknowledged the dispatcher as I drove expeditiously to assist the officer. *La Colonia* was a high-crime area and I took the call seriously. As I arrived, I did not see the officer's unit anywhere near. I was surprised that I had arrived first although I had been several miles away.

When the dispatched officer finally arrived—without, I might add, an excuse for being late—I told him that we should check out the roof. After climbing up, I saw a person coming out of the drugstore's skylight with a bag. He spotted me and started running. At that moment I yelled to the Beat 2 Officer, "The suspect is on the roof. Climb up!" I had reached the roof by climbing a chain-link fence and expected my fellow officer to do the same, but he did not. I chased the suspect, keeping him in view as he ran toward a nearby building. I looked back for my partner. He wasn't in sight. I did not want the suspect to get away.

I continued running after the suspect until my legs got tangled in a knot of TV antenna wires. I hit the roof hard with both knees. I felt a sharp pain in my right knee. I felt, almost with detached fascination, as the pain rapidly became unbearable. I knew within a few moments that I could no longer stand up. The suspect noticed that I had fallen down, and he started running back toward me. I could see his body with the help of my flashlight. As the suspect drew near, his body got bigger and bigger until it was an impossible size. He was huge, toned, and muscular. When he drew to within eight yards of me, I pulled my handgun out of my holster and yelled, "Stop! If you take another step, I'll blow you away!"

I made certain that the suspect could see my handgun by using my flashlight. He didn't move. "Turn around!" I yelled. He complied. "I do not want you to move an inch," I yelled at him. "Lie face down on the roof!" Again, he complied. He had no idea that my legs were tangled up in wires. I told him to place his hands behind his back, but he did not follow my orders. I rolled over to where he was, got on his back, placed my weapon behind his head, and said, "What you are feeling on the back of your head is my gun. It might go off if you move a whisker, so don't." I started with his left arm. When I grabbed his bicep I noticed that it was bigger than a cantaloupe. "Oh Lord," I thought. "Help me get out of this one. Give me the strength and courage to defeat my enemy."

The suspect's left wrist was too big for my handcuff. I was barely able to force it to the first click. I then ordered him to place his right arm behind his back, and he refused. He pretended that he could not do it due to the extra muscle he had on his bicep.

I repeated myself: "If you move, I'll blow your brains out." I had no choice; he was not cooperating with me, and the Beat 2 Officer never climbed up on the roof to assist me. I was upset with my partner, to say the least. I could have used his help dealing with this 6' 2" monster. I kept on telling the giant to place his right arm on his back, and he started complaining that I was hurting his left arm as I pulled the handcuff ring in an attempt to catch his right wrist. I propped the handle of my gun against the back of his neck and rested the barrel against his head. It was now or never. I repeated my comment not to move, let go of the gun, and grabbed his right arm quickly. If he moves, the gun will drop and then he'll kill me, I thought.

I was lucky that night. I had the suspect always looking the opposite direction of the arm I was going to handcuff, and he never knew what was going on. The suspect didn't move a whisker, and I was able to quickly grab his right arm and force my handcuff on his right wrist. I strained until I heard the first click, the sweetest sound I had ever heard. I had him. I removed the wires from my legs and stood up by supporting my body with the suspect's. I was limping as we walked toward the edge of the building. My knee was screaming in agony. By this time, several officers had arrived at the scene, and officer Adcock from Beat 3 helped me get down from the roof.

We arrived at the police station to book the suspect. I had to leave soon, but not before a checkup of my injury. Before I left, Officer Adcock ran a computer check on the suspect and told me that the man I had just caught burglarizing had "escaped a week ago from a state prison in Northern California." He had seriously injured (or killed) two deputy sheriffs in the process, a feat that was not difficult for me to believe.

I never found out what happened to the Beat 2 officer. I believe he wrote the report, which was the least he could have done. Several officers had warned me about this officer's attitude in the field and told me that whenever he received life-threatening calls, he would always make sure to arrive last. I did not believe them at the time, but he proved them to be correct. Was this officer, a big man (6'2", 220 pounds) a coward? I have no idea, but he behaved very unprofessionally on that call. However, after this incident, I never trusted this person as a reliable back-up officer and I lost respect for him.

On numerous occasions afterward, I saw him writing his police reports while parked in front of his home, outside of the city's limits, instead of writing them in an area where he could be attentive to his job. There are, unfortunately, always one or two people in any organization with this type of unreliability.

Officer Down

One warm summer evening, I was patrolling Beat 2 in the downtown area. This was a bar and restaurant area where drug sales were common. I noticed a parked vehicle in a vacant lot adjacent to a fast-food restaurant. I thought I had seen some type of movement in the vehicle. I stopped in the middle of the street and observed again. Yes, there was movement inside the vehicle. It wasn't obvious, but I decided to check it out. I quickly parked my car and reported my location to the dispatcher: "Station 1, 2 Charles, will check suspicious movement in a car, vacant lot between Fifth and Meta Street."

"10-4, 2 Charles," responded the dispatcher.

I approached the vehicle. There was a man attempting to rape a blonde woman.

Acting instinctively, I quickly opened the driver's side door. As I started to pull the man out, I was hit in the face. The suspect knocked me flat on my back on the ground. I remember that he attempted to run, and I grabbed his legs and pulled him to the ground. We struggled for a while, and the next thing I remember was being hit on the head. I heard a thick, dull thud each time the suspect hit me. I had dropped my sixteen-inch steel police flashlight after I was hit the first time, and the suspect had picked it up. As my vision began to blur, I attempted to put a chokehold on the suspect. He bit me on the right wrist. I tried again, and this time he bit me on the right bicep. I was grabbing the suspect wherever I could. I was desperate to make certain that he did not get away from me.

As our struggle continued, the victim attempted to help me, but to no avail. She was in my way at times, running around us, screaming, crying. She was yelling for people in the area to help. She picked up my police radio from the ground and yelled for help. I attempted to give her instructions to get the SOS out. We continued struggling; I could hear again and again that same thud as the flashlight collided with my skull. I was getting dizzy. Black and reddish colors reeled through my mind. I was about to pass out, but somehow I remained fix-ated. I kept telling myself that this guy was not getting away from me. I'll never know how, but I was able to grab my handcuffs and place one ring tight on his wrist and one on mine. I passed out. Reality came and went. I remember his carrying me as I phased in and out of consciousness.

"I have to keep conscious." The thought repeated in my mind.

I woke to the voice of Officer Mike Alford. He was attempting to carry me to his patrol unit. He kept on asking me for my name as he drove to St. John's Hospital. "Stay awake, Mickey." That was his nickname for me - Mickey. He was driving fast, everything was fading to black, he was yelling at me continu-ously, willing me to stay awake. I remember passing out a couple of times in the back seat and hearing a voice call from far away. "Mickey, Mickey, don't go out on me, buddy." I remember not being able to breathe…

I woke up in the hospital.

Everything changed from that night onward. I spent the next eight months in and out of hospitals. I suffered from intense headaches and dizzy spells. I began taking all types of medication. To make matters worse, I began to receive ill-intentioned responses from the city risk management office. "Do what you want," they told me whenever I called their office to discuss which doctors I could see. I returned to patrol several times and took office assignments, but I kept having debilitating headaches. And to make my problem worse, I was con-stantly harassed by a lieutenant because I was taking prescribed medication. He would yell derogatory things like "When the hell are you going out to patrol, Pinzón?" I filed a complaint against him, but nothing happened. He contin-ued his harassment for moths. The lieutenant's belligerent attitude and constant pressure were so overwhelming that at times I felt he was attempting to force me to quit the police department. This man endeavored to make me feel worthless and guilty for getting hurt on the job. I never understood his attitude toward me.

I felt humiliated. The city government that I had worked for loyally had betrayed me. Many police officers today throughout the county continue to undergo the same things I did when they get injured on the job. I had to fight my own employers for justice, as though the criminals on the streets were not enough to deal with. I had one desire that trumped all others--I wanted to return to patrol! I wanted to get well and return to the work I loved, and the people I loved to serve. The city expected me to be cured as though it were like snapping your fingers. I asked myself if my poor treatment was due to "racism". Did they think I was a Mexican who had come to this country as a child and wanted an easy retirement; who wanted to return to his "home country" and live in style on American dollars? The continual abuse eventually became unbearable. With a great weight in my heart, I left law enforcement forever.

The suspect who had assaulted me went to jail and came out too soon. He later battered another police officer and almost injured a third one. But during the last altercation, he was shot. An Oxnard sergeant told me this years later.

Our job as police officers is complicated. We go out into the streets every day, on or off duty, not knowing if we will be returning home to our families. Our blood pressure goes haywire every time we receive a call. We also develop a keen understanding of human nature because we must be ready to take on many roles during our shifts. We are psychologists, counselors, friends, fathers, nurses, lawyers; and police officers. Our main concern is to protect our citizens, our cities, and ultimately, our way of life.

Far too often city administrators lose the perspective of our purpose due to the pull of politicking and other narrow interests. City administrators cannot forget our heroes in blue who give their lives every day hold the spirit of our Constitution with every fiber of their being. Yet there is an endless, unseen toll created by the work of these brave men in uniform.

I spent months in and out of hospitals and never recuperated fully. But I had to count my blessings. "I am alive," I would repeat to myself over and over. In the time I remained on the force after my injury, an officer was killed in the line of duty. He was shot with a .22 caliber weapon during a domestic dispute call he was handling. One of my beloved sergeants passed on, and a young former officer committed suicide. One does not know what will happen under the stressful circumstances a police officer endures.

After leaving law enforcement, I returned to the Oxnard Police Department several times to see Officer Stofey. The last time I spoke with Robert, on the day before his retirement dinner, he said, "Miguel, it was a good thing that you left the police department when you did. A few high-brass people didn't like you at all. They were afraid of you because you were too educated. Leaving the department was the best thing for you. They were out to get you, and you left just in time." I thanked him for everything he had done for me. That was the last time I saw my trusted friend Robert.

During my convalescence I made plans to move to Hawaii and set up an export and import business from Asia to the Americas. I also wanted to open a Mexican food restaurant, but I was still having terrible headaches and I did not have any medical coverage or money. I could not afford my plans, and I did not want to sell my home; thus, I decided to move to Cuernavaca, Mexico, for a while, where my brother-in-law was going to provide free medical assistance.

As I was saying my good-byes at the police station, a friend at the Oxnard Police Department whose husband had been killed in the line of duty as a Los Angeles police officer in the 1960s said to me, "Once a cop, always a cop." She was right. That strong desire to protect the innocent and expose those who are corrupt in spirit and abuse the weak has always stayed in my heart.

During my years as a police officer, I was enrolled in a M.A. in Management program at the University of Redlands. I had finished all my courses in the program but was not able to finish my thesis in those years due to health issues. Nevertheless, I had learned many management and financial concepts that later helped me in the next chapter of my life.

CHAPTER 6

Corporate Man

Efficiency is doing things right; effectiveness is doing the right thing.

Peter Drucker

Johnson & Johnson

When I arrived in Mexico City in late 1981, I met John Smith, a young man from Kansas who was working as a headhunter. I made contact with him through a newspaper ad. Dow Chemical was attempting to fill a labor relations position for their Latin American operations. He thought I had an excellent resume and set me up to interview for the job. I passed two directors' interviews. In those interviews I established excellent rapport, but in my final and last interview, I could not reach an agreement with a third director. He was snobbish, and I did not like his arrogant attitude. Twenty minutes or so into our conversation, I thanked him for the opportunity and left his office. I was not interested in working for someone like him, especially when he told me that I was going to be reporting to him.

I kept in contact with John. For some time I had had a gut feeling that he was using a fictitious name. I finally told him what I thought. A week later, after John got to know me a bit more and we had started to become friends, he gave me a response. "You're right, Miguel, my name is fictitious, and I've used this name since I started working in Mexico because I did not get a job permit." John and other friends from New York had been working in the country illegally for about a year.

In the following days, I interviewed at the Ortho Diagnostics Division of Johnson & Johnson (J&J). I was eventually hired as a sales manager and given a month of training. After finishing the program, I was placed in charge of the central region of the country. My position covered six states. J&J had a strict business ethics policy, and that was one of the key factors our sales force had over most of our competition—we didn't bribe anybody to influence our sales or to win contests for national government bids.

Our blood typing screening products were of such high quality that they could have sold themselves. I was proud to work in a company where bribery was not a custom. This was refreshing in light of the way a lot of other sales people and multinational corporations behaved. Private distributors and the Instituto Mexicano del Seguro Social (Mexican Institute of Social Security), our strongest client, trusted our products—and us.

My office base was in Leon, Guanajuato, which was situated near the beautiful village of San Miguel de Allende. I wanted only committed and quality people to be in my team. I did not care about university degrees; I had seen too many professionals who were committed only to making money, who did not care about their team members or the company. I wanted people who had a desire to work as a team and wanted to sell our product with passion. I wanted people who were inspired to become important members of our organization.

I wanted loyalty. Yes, they were going to make money, something that I strongly supported, but I did not want them to earn it by deceiving and lying to our customers. We had the best products on the market. It was now up to us to effectively promote our products.

I introduced myself to all the owners of the distribution centers in my area and their working teams. I met the sales force one by one, and after observing them for a few days, I gave them courses in sales skills, business ethics, and customer service. I established my credibility with all the distributors and the sales force and learned about the different issues they had with J&J. I took a personal approach to my job. I was constantly in touch with every sales person. I met all of their clients and learned about their business and personal expectations. I asked them what they expected from me, and I told them what I expected from them. I set up different policies that were crucial in creating a positive working environment. I wanted to increase sales and needed everyone to be well trained and motivated. In order to accomplish these goals, I drew up a list of eight policies:

1. Personnel were to be efficient during their eight-hour workdays. No one was to work a minute longer except in the case of an emergency. I wanted each employee to spend quality time with his or her family. I reasoned that if they were okay with their families, they were going to be okay at work.

2. I would lend the best sales person of the week my company car for the weekend as a bonus. All of the sales personnel used public transportation to visit clients; none of them had a personal car. This bonus motivated the sales force, and sales increased dramatically within three months. I was later assigned two more states and fifty percent of Mexico City thanks to the results we had in my area.

3. Everyone had to establish credibility and leadership with his or her clients. The sale personnel were never to promise a customer anything that could not be delivered on time.

4. Every sales person had to teach our customers about why our J&J products were better than the competition. This usually involved presenting reports on the depth of our quality and the advantages and strengths we possessed over all the other products on the market.

5. Sales people were to assure clients that we cared for them and that our team was going to be with them in any circumstance.

6. I would do everything possible to make the personnel in the sales force feel good about themselves, and I would never place myself as an unquestionable authority above my teams. I would listen to their suggestions and comments. I would make myself available to all of them whenever they needed me.

7. We had to work as a team. We worked together because we had a company goal. We had to reach that goal first. Personal goals were a second priority.

8. Good work was to be praised, and mistakes were to be corrected.

I traveled constantly in my area, often covering over one thousand miles per week. This caused some difficulties since I also needed to be near my doctors. My headaches hadn't stopped. I kept my health a secret from J&J. During the hiring process, I had passed a minimal health examination that consisted of blood tests. They were administered by an MD who represented Johnson & Johnson. He did not detect anything wrong with me.

We made great progress in my area. According to the director, this was something that J&J had not done in previous years. I was happy with what I had accomplished with my team. Our sales continued to grow, and our team was developing remarkably.

In this same time period, I was involved in a near-fatal car accident. I passed out while driving and drove into the back end of a double-carriage semi-truck, with my vehicle ended up underneath it. The company's car was almost demolished, and the top half was destroyed. By some miracle I was unharmed. I didn't even have a scratch. When the highway patrolman saw the vehicle, he said that I was lucky that my head had not been cut off by the impact. It went without saying. I saw the damage done to the car and could not believe I had walked away with my life.

A few months later, I resigned from J&J. My sales team gave me a dinner party in one of their homes. All of their families came together, and we said good-bye. Many were very sentimental and thanked me. I had never had so many people show so much care and love for me. I was overwhelmed. I was proud of the team I had developed. I had worked for an excellent multinational company and learned many things during my short stay there, but I could not travel anymore. My headaches were occurring more frequently. My past injury was catching up to me, and I did not want the company to know. I had to be near the doctors who were taking care of me in Cuernavaca, five hundred miles away.

Setting up Networks

Three months after my resignation from J&J, I was hired at Kladt/GIK Corporation, a plastics manufacturing group in Cuernavaca. My starting position was that of logistics assistant manager. Within four months I was promoted to the position of Strategic Planning, Logistics & Inventory Manager. I did not need to take any health tests for this company, and was only given a psychological test. At this company, we produced a wide variety of plastic products. We made small plastic bottles for eye drops, oil barrels for Pemex, the Trac II cartridges for Gillette, and numerous bottles for multinationals. All in all, we manufactured over 350 different plastic products. We had three distribution centers in the country—in Monterrey, Guadalajara, and Mexico City.

Our plant director and co-owner, J. Kladt, an engineer, two other production engineers, two manufacturing supervisors, a maintenance supervisor, and our team made our group one of the top plastic bottle producers in the country within sixteen months. According to a business magazine at the time, we were one of the top three plastic companies in the country, if not number one. We were very proud of having accomplished that task by working as a team. Our director strutted like a peacock for a couple of years and started calling me "doctor," although I had not received that academic degree yet.

The company was having serious management problems at the time of my hiring. The different department directors seemed to be in constant discord over how the production line was to be managed. The director of sales and marketing was micromanaging, and was allowed to do so due to the personal relationship she had with an owner-director. She kept giving orders to the production director as to what should be produced. This constant change in production orders wound up adversely affecting the morale and production output of plant personnel and caused delivery delays. This all led to higher costs. The company's financial and organizational management was in a constant state of chaos. There were many debts and no money to purchase raw materials. Many promised bonuses were not paid to managers, but only to a privileged few, or partial bonus payments were made as though they were supposed to be given in installments.

During my first week at the company, the production director and an assistant (his brother) were fired. Apparently they had clashed with the union leaders. The production line employees continued working for about five months after this and then went on a three-month strike. Prior to the strike, I had created good relations with the union leaders and all the employees. I tried to persuade them to stop the strike. My words had no effect. However, prior to the strike, I had established strategies for my department so our working relationships with the finance, production, quality control, and sales personnel would not be affected if a strike occurred.

At the same time, I had to keep abreast of the production output, inventories, invoices, and all of the purchasing deliveries owed to customers in the country. My key responsibility was to coordinate all the departments concerned so that production was steady and products were delivered to our customers. We established a Just in Time program. Within a few months, I had also established a network with different managers at Pond's (now Unilever), Alucaps, and other multinational organizations in CIVAC, Cuernavaca's Industrial Park area.

My relationships with individuals continued to improve, which helped everyone in our network improve our production efficiency through borrowing one another's equipment and raw materials and sometimes sharing technical know-how when anyone needed it. To give an example, there were times that the raw material delivery truck was parked outside our company waiting for the order from headquarters in Mexico City. They would not unload the material until we had paid. Sometimes our company did not have the funds to pay at the time of delivery. This happened often enough that I had to create strong mutual understandings with neighboring company managers. We developed a powerful business bond. This strategy helped prevent production stoppages caused by a lack of raw material. When the strike hit us we were ready. We had surplus inventory ready for delivery and for incoming orders.

Also in anticipation of a future strike, the plant director had rented a warehouse, and my department was in charge of taking the entire inventory out of our plant to the warehouse, where it was made ready to be delivered to our customers when they placed orders. I used our own transportation for deliveries to Mexico City and negotiated with freight truck owners to give me credit on other freights to different places in the country. I succeeded in negotiating a seven-to-fifteen-day credit line with each owner, and sometimes I renegotiated an extension to thirty days. These negotiations gave us cash that we used to alleviate other problems.

During the third week of the strike, the sales and marketing director started giving orders to my personnel as to when deliveries were to be made. She constantly attempted to challenge my authority. When I spoke to my boss, the plant director, about the incident, I said, "I can't work with people who want to micromanage my department, especially when that individual doesn't have a clue about management principles."

I continued, "I know how to do my job well. I've done a good job so far, considering the strike." I further stated that, "I recently worked for an important multinational company, where I was trained well and had excellent results. I have experience and management education. I'm not going to work for mediocre family companies where a director can do as she pleases. The only person who is going to give me orders is you." After finishing my tirade, I waited for the plant director to fire me. I was upset because the sales director had lied to my personnel and treated them without respect. On several occasions she held up deliveries to Mexico City because she had not closed a deal properly, or wanted us to deliver products ahead of time. These problems had existed for some time. I wanted our company to operate as a professional business, not as a family business where orders were changed constantly. The sales director and her personnel were paid a bonus if they met their monthly sales goals. The early delivery tactic was a disreputable way to reach the sales quota. These tactics increased our costs tremendously and created a drag on overall efficiency.

I continued telling the plant director that I was going to resign once the strike was over if the situation with the sales director was not resolved. He asked me to stay because he liked the quality of my work and wanted me in his company. Kladt convinced me that he was going to back me up in all my decisions. I was not willing to cover other people's mistakes or allow my personnel to be inconvenienced or angered by the mistakes of other departments. I was not going to tolerate the inefficiencies, or personal agendas, that had persisted for too long.

I agreed to continue working for him, but I stated specifically, "I am not going to take orders from the sales and marketing director, only from you. In my department I am the only one who is responsible if something goes wrong, and I alone give orders." He agreed with me. Once the strike was over, half of the production employees were laid off, and the rest of the personnel returned to the plant. All the departments had been separated and were working in two different places in the city.

Once we returned to our plant, we set up a new management concept for doing business and established new procedures. Our policies and leadership style prevailed for over three years. I received excellent practical experience as I involved myself in every department, from finance and purchasing, to quality control and production. This was invaluable in helping us reach our real monthly production and sales goals. I kept weekly, and sometimes daily, statistical reports and graphs of our production, sales, production rejections, and real delivery costs.

A key policy we followed involved keeping our personnel motivated and committed to the company. We were obsessed with maintaining a continual learning process and retraining our personnel. We also gave our people inspirational mini-talks to help them reach their potential. I spoke to my employees about the importance of being efficient and did not deceive them, as the previous production director had had. I treated them with respect and dignity. The plant director was pleased with our progress.

Unfortunately the good times could not last forever. The plant director transferred out to seek further business endeavors in the United States. His departure had a definite negative effect on our team. Many changes were made at the plant. The new plant director began playing politics with the other department directors. Hardly anyone cared for his new policies. Eventually all the managers left to find new endeavors.

I kept going. I thought that I could persuade the production director to establish "management by objectives" strategies in order to establish bonuses for the employees, but he did not care. The plant director did not have our company's goal as his first priority. It seemed to us that he was more concerned with making money for his outsourcing company that gave us second process service. His impersonal, avaricious attitude was destroying our employee motivation. Many times they were forced to work twice on the same product, at times with no extra pay.

I had previously established a policy with my personnel that if I won, everybody won. If our department reached our monthly goal and I received a bonus, so did my employees. The bonus policy was cancelled entirely once the new plant director took reign of the company. My subordinates, who were understandably upset to have their bonuses taken away, criticized me unfairly. They accused me of receiving my bonus and not sharing it with them.

From this point on, the company started to lose clients. Quality control began to decline, and our products were constantly being rejected. Our clients stopped trusting us. A new production manager took over but could not prevent a decline in both personnel synergy and our market share. At times, I was ordered to deliver products even though the new production director knew that it was of poor quality or the wrong color. When I was away from the plant, my personnel were given orders to do things that contradicted my goals and commitment to superior work. The new directors did not care about the principles we had cultivated with Kladt. I felt used by the directors after Kladt left the company. I had little real power. To make matters worse, I caught typhoid and was absent from work for a month. After I returned, the new production director made decisions that affected my integrity. I resigned two weeks later.

The new production manager slowly destroyed what we had put together over the course of four long years: worker faith in an employee-oriented, highly democratic work system. Our organizational culture had been completely altered. Everything was in shambles. My employees would tell me they wanted to leave the company. I had to advise them against this course of action because I knew how difficult it would be for them to find new work. It was 1986, and there was a recession in the country. There were no jobs for college graduates, let alone those who, like most of my workers, did not have an elementary or secondary school education. I had an opportunity to work for Givaudan, an industrial Swiss manufacturer of fragrances and flavorings. They were located only a block away from where I worked, but I wanted to think about my future before taking a job in another company and continuing as a corporate man.

In 1986, I returned home to California. I needed to make new plans for my future. I decided to start a business where I could institute my philosophy of doing business. I was going to hire people who believed in commitment, had a sense of responsibility and sound ethics, and strongly believed in teamwork and customer service. I wanted people who were willing to learn and were passionate about their work and the impact it would have.

CHAPTER 7

An Entrepreneur

---◆◆◆---

*Neither studies nor market research nor computer
modeling are a substitute for the test of reality.*

Peter Drucker

During the mid-eighties, I started several small businesses. I also made a series of sound stock investments. I constantly argued with my brokers because they did not want to follow my instructions when I asked them to buy and sell shares. My dreams for life were beginning to come true, and this, in turn, allowed me to work with the poor more intensely and assist them in creating a better life for their families. Everything I touched turned to gold. I was immensely grateful to God for my good fortune.

I had decided to walk away from the corporate world. There was too much politicking and too many violations committed by profit-hungry directors. Only the strong survived, and if you knew how to manipulate the social realm, you could someday become a top director in these companies, I thought. I was not interested because some of their politics involved dishonorable actions. My idea of business is being interested in creating employment opportunities, not laying people off to increase profit margins.

In today's business world, recent graduates want to become the boss during their first years. They do not want to be an employee. They aren't aware that learning to manage a business and people is a process. I do not have the talent to play politics and was never very good at kissing up to unscrupulous or arrogant bosses. I admit that I am a proud person with unshakeable self-dignity, but I am not arrogant—at least I try not to be. My pride involves being productive and responsible to my employees and to society.

I am an idealistic person, but I'm realistic. I have seen great ignorance in many individuals, especially those who are possessed by a negative attitude. Maybe they became frustrated with their dreams somewhere along the line, and they became angry for one reason or another and stopped growing. Even so, through education or training, work, and a strong will, dreams can become a reality. Additionally, I strongly believe that ignorance and poor academic preparation hold back personal development. I kept these ideas in mind as I planned my business strategy. I wanted forward-looking, enthusiastic people who were willing to develop our company, to be in tune with our team.

In the mid-1900s Joseph Schumpeter warned that the bureaucratization of capitalism was going to destroy the spirit of entrepreneurship. He believed in a concept of "creative destruction" in which products and ideas had to be destroyed and renewed constantly. This concept has become especially important in today's world of constant crisis. Since President Ronald Reagan revolutionized economics in the 1980s, governments, businesses, and universities of almost every ideological outlook have embraced entrepreneurship. The United Nations, the European Union, and the World Bank have also become addicted to this concept. Entrepreneurship has been born again. I decided to jump on the bandwagon.

I decided to become an entrepreneur. By owning my own small business, I could establish my own policies and procedures. I wanted to innovate on my concept of business management. I had experimented with different management models of my own devising at both Johnson & Johnson and at Kladt/GIK Corp. I knew exactly what I wanted to do and knew my management style, but I needed to improve it. I recognized, however, that my expertise in small business would come only with more experience. I wanted to create a business where employees were trained properly, paid a just wage, and could make more money if they applied themselves to growing the business.

It was time to bring my idea to life. I had witnessed too many broken promises by different corporations. I had witnessed corporate managers and business owners who did not pay bonuses promised to employees or who paid the minimum wage and benefits established by law to their employees although these companies had excellent profits. Worse, they did this to employees who were below the poverty line. I knew there was a better way and that it was within my power to make it a reality.

THE HELL WITH CIRCUMSTANCES; I WILL CREATE MY OWN JOB
OPPORTUNITIES IN LIFE.

Trust Is the Key

I wanted my employees to trust me. In order to do that, I had to deliver on what I had promised them. However, they had to share the responsibility by managing their own departments efficiently. This involved keeping costs low by using raw materials efficiently, reaching sales objectives, and giving proper service to customers in order to secure their loyalty to our company. A strong commitment to these policies was going to be the key to our success.

My employees were the soul of my business. I believed that employees had to be trained because they were the ones who faced our customers directly, produced or sold our products, and helped manage the business by providing the proper information when requested. Several strategies I had learned in the two corporations I had worked for were to teach my employees to see our customers as our business partners, to be innovative throughout the company, to keep our costs down, to give the best quality on the market, and to have a fair price.

Most importantly, we did sales follow-up, a concept that I had applied at J&J. This would generally involve calling the customers once a month, or more often if necessary, to see if they were satisfied with our products and to ask if they needed to place any additional orders. If so, the product was to be delivered at no extra charge. I had applied all these strategies in the past, and I was successful. Now, I needed to convince my people to believe in my dream and to make it their own.

In 1986 I started an import-export business with an associate. We searched for the best-handcrafted items in all of Mexico, from the northernmost state of the country, Sonora, to the south in Oaxaca. I visited many family businesses in different villages until I found items that met my standard of quality and output. We were going to distribute our products in California, Florida, Georgia, and Holland.

We also started a dental supply business and made many deals for dental equipment in the United States, Mexico, and Germany. Consequently, in 1987, I started a chain of pharmaceutical stores with my doctor brother-in-law. This venture, in addition to being profitable, allowed me to help the poor. In time I was able to open a medical clinic with four associate medical doctors, friends of mine, who saw to the needs experienced by poor families. I started to become more involved with children suffering from brain dystrophy. I discovered that the Children's Rehabilitation Center in Cuernavaca (CRIC) needed funds to buy medicine and would donate to them whatever I could when needed.

The pharmaceutical business was gradually growing. I spent fourteen hours a day, seven days a week, managing it. They were long hours, but we needed to develop the business into what I wanted it to become. After several months, I had asked my subordinates to take care of the business while I spent more time volunteering at the CRIC. I had agreed with my employees that I would cover the business by myself every evening between 7:00 and 11:00 p.m. I opened every day at 8:00 a.m. and spent all Sunday in the business.

We had negotiated an excellent discount of 35% from our suppliers, thirty days credit, and a special price whenever we purchased volume, such as buying 25,000 of a specific product and receiving 10,000 free. These negotiations allowed for our success, as we were able to offer especially low prices to our customers. Sales increased. At the same time, in the late 1980s and 1990s, I was also involved with other businesses in California with my mother and a younger sister. We had a grocery store and care homes for people whose health had been affected by drug use.

By summer 1992, I had been in businesses eleven years and felt that I had learned a great deal about the discipline of business management. It was time to give back. I wanted to offer my knowledge to students. I was hired at the Tec de Monterrey campus Cuernavaca to teach an entrepreneurship course as an adjunct professor and was highly evaluated by my students. As entrepreneurs, we make many costly mistakes in our first start-ups and I wanted to teach young university students how to avoid them. I wanted them to learn from my experience, so they could become better managers.

When entrepreneurs make mistakes, these errors have a high cost that most people and organizations cannot afford to waste, especially in today's business climate. The Small Business Management (2012), and The Small Business Entrepreneurship Council (2014) indicated that seven out of ten new businesses survived their initial two years; 45 percent businesses fail in the first five years in the USA. Presently, 80 percent of businesses fail in first two years in Latin America. The key reasons for business failure are insufficient funds, lack of management skills, lack of selling skills, and lack of publicity. Entrepreneurs must learn to be innovative and must constantly be searching for new ways of doing business efficiently and effectively.

Young entrepreneurs must become wiser, good leaders, managers and negotiators who are responsible to our communities and the environment; and, I

MY LIFE: WHAT A LIFE

pray, become highly ethical and better human beings. I have a very strong commitment when I teach. I want my students to become true entrepreneurs, business people who will make money but will be responsible to their employees, their communities, and to the world, so they can make it a better place for us all and future generations. I strongly believe that a business professor should combine lectures about what he or she has done in the real business world with management theory concepts in order to bring the students to the real world of business.

Living the Dream

In November 1992, I met Mario Lembo, an Italian count who spent most of his time in Cuernavaca but also lived in New York and in Rome. He wanted to invest $300,000 in the stock market and asked me if I could advise him. Mario told me that he had heard about me in a business conference I had given at a university, and he liked my ideas. We had never formally met, although for some time he had been a neighbor who lived three houses away from me. He was a tall, handsome man in his younger years, always wearing a suit and tie regardless of where he was going, whether it was the local market, a luncheon, or the movies. He was a reserved and religious person who generally kept to himself in our neighborhood.

The count had chosen to live in Cuernavaca permanently since 1985. Many Europeans had lived there since the 1940s. International movie stars also made their summer home in Cuernavaca, as well as well-known global dignitaries and famous authors. At one point Gloria Swanson, John Wayne and California's Governor Jerry Brown also made their home in "the city of eternal spring."

I did research for about two weeks and told Mario to invest in San Luis and Peñoles, Mexican mining stocks. A month later, after taking my advice, Mario invited me to his home. We met there every Wednesday evening thereafter from 8:00 p.m. to 11:00 p.m. to talk about business or whatever he had in mind. We became excellent friends as the years passed. During this time, he offered me an unexpected gift: a castle his family had received from the Italian royalty outside of Rome. This castle was given to his family by the king many years ago."

He had inherited it in the 1950s. Now that he was growing older, he felt that I should have it as a reward for all the help I had given him without any pay. Mario's great-great-grandfather had been the king's fencing instructor; thus, the Italian nobility respected his family.

Through Mario, I gradually became involved with a "royalty group," as I called them. The count told them that he had profited close to $1,000,000 within two years and that I had recuperated over $500,000 that he had almost lost in an investment in Texas. Mario was an excellent opera singer. He had been good friends with Josephine Baker, the American singer living in France, and sang with her in a few shows in Paris. I attended many exuberant, tasteful parties at Mario's home. Bacchus, the god of wine, gave us many liters of his divine drink, and it was the center around which many business gatherings and business meetings revolved. The count was also a devoted religious man who had adopted several indigent Mexican children. He eventually returned them to their parents since he felt it was best for them to live at home.

When Mario turned seventy, he invited my family and me to his party, where many important people from European royalty were present. He also introduced me to a group of his friends. I later became their business advisor and started financing small businesses. All the members of this group lived in Cuernavaca and would spend three to six months of the year in Europe, Palm Beach, Florida, or Manhattan, New York, depending upon their personal commitments.

I started advising European royalty—three Italian counts, a former Russian princess—and a prominent American businessman who lived in Cuernavaca. Within two years, I made a substantial amount of money for the group in several businesses and in the stock market. Due to the constant ups and downs in the market, I decided to create a pool with their money. I started investing in different countries around the world, buying into sixty-three small companies as a venture capitalist. I would research the best places to invest in small businesses so they could grow, set up my tried-and-tested rules, and started the business. Our business grew tremendously until the venture came to an end in 2002, when a few members of the investment group passed away. I continued on my own.

Our success emanated not only from doing the right deal but also from executing and keeping our promises with our employees, business alliances, and customers. Our investments, ideas on growth, and ability to find products and markets helped us create a proper relationship-building approach that may not necessarily have had any immediate financial value but proved to be a major source for our overall global success. I found business partners who opened doors for us, and in turn, we capitalized on these networks and achieved joint profits.

Do not let all the above deceive you, however. Money, while unquestionably important, does not bring me happiness or make me a successful person by itself. I feel successful when I feel reciprocated and deserving of love from my family and friends. I feel successful when I can give hope to someone who needs my help, when I can create happiness for the poor and help them regain their dignity. I feel successful when I see children smile because there is food on their table. I feel successful when I have done everything possible not to harm anybody either directly or indirectly.

But living in different places grows tiresome. In 2008, after twenty-seven years of itinerant living, my wife, my daughter, and I attempted to make our permanent residence in Manhattan, where I had been living on a part-time basis since 1997-'98. While there, I had an interview to be an adjunct professor at Columbia University. I was given an appointment date to meet the business professor with whom I had been in touch since 2002. Finally, my appointment date arrived; it was a cold, snowy day. As I walked into his office, he said, "I always wanted to meet that man who travels around the world" for the sake of business. He asked me to tell him everything about the things I had done in twenty minutes because he had another meeting, so I spoke hastily, just to satisfy his curiosity. I told him about some of my experiences. I felt that I was wasting my time talking to him, but I finished sharing part of my experiences in business.

I could not believe what I heard after I finished my brief story. In a very eloquent manner, he stated, "You will never teach here. You should apply at a junior college. You might get a job there, but not at Columbia." I felt that I had returned to 1973 when I met, for the first time, an arrogant college professor.

Although I had almost thirty years of practical world business experience, had provided mentoring and created a successful network of investors; although I had attracted customers and made partners in many businesses worldwide, had years of excellent professorship evaluations from top universities and several academic degrees, an MBA from the University of Redlands in California, a Master's in applied economics, and two PhDs—one in entrepreneurship and family business from a top European university—I was not good enough for Columbia?

"Wow, Zeus, the god from Mount Olympus, has spoken and given his verdict," I thought. Yes, people can have their own prejudices, but to be ill-mannered is another matter entirely. I had never been offended this way since my junior college years. He had insulted my intelligence, but I wanted to laugh. He then attempted to bring civility back into the conversation by asking me if he could give me suggestions on how to improve my resume. I went along with his suggestion and thanked him. I did not want to lower myself to his level and did not ask him why he had made that comment. I left his office wondering what he wanted to prove or what his point was in telling me what he did.

It wasn't all bad, however. I had a great time visiting the campus. For a couple of hours, I spoke with several students from different parts of the country and the world about international entrepreneurship development. As the Dalai Lama once said, "Forget about the negativisms you encounter in the world; don't worry about superficial people or things in the world." And so I did.

WHEN I SPEAK OF HAPPINESS AND BEING SUCCESSFUL,
I REFER TO AN INNER PEACE, WHICH SHOWS ITSELF ON
OUR FACES, IN OUR ATTITUDE AND LOVE FOR OTHERS

CHAPTER 8

Twenty-First Century: Entrepreneurship Must Go Forward

Leaders set people's spirits free, often inspiring them to become more than they ever thought possible, and encourage them to [become more innovated and productive].

Author Unknown

The Internet, eBay auctions, mobile phones, and nanotechnology are some of the innovations that have created the greatest opportunities we have seen that provide real, value-added products and services to consumers and businesses worldwide—giving instant information which brings the consumer closer to the entrepreneur.

From Muhammad Yunus, "The Banker to the Poor", a designation in which he takes great pride (The Grameen Family Companies); Jack Ma, Alibaba Group, genius Chinese entrepreneur; Oprah Winfrey with her conglomerate; Bill Gates (Microsoft); Mark Zuckerburg (Facebook); Lorenzo Servitje (Bimbo); and Amancio Ortega (Zara)—these are entrepreneurs who continuously developed products and services so compelling that consumers want them. Furthermore, each of these new products or services has created entire industries of support products. However, for today's entrepreneurs, the past years of innovations have created the greatest economic opportunity in history because there are so many ready-to-be-implemented business opportunities in practically every sector of the world economy.

What happened in the first decade of the 21st century? Between 2000 and 2008, our economy grew, as measured by gross domestic product indicators, from \$9.8 trillion to about \$14.5 trillion. This resulted in an enormous boost in consumer disposable income from investments, wages, and purchasing power. Traditionally, when economic output rises, people's lifestyles improve. Many world consumers purchased more luxurious products, expensive automobiles, new electronic devices including iPads and cell phones, fancier homes, and went on more world trips.

As an example, the average price paid for a single-family home in the United States was \$195,000 in 2000. This jumped to \$320,000 in 2008, with a decrease of 20 to 45 percent from 2009 to 2011; and again increased in January 2015 to the highest level since August 2013, according to the National Association of Realtors. Miami realtors indicated the median price of a con-dominium in the Miami-Dade area rose about 20 percent in 2014; and that of a single-family home jumped 16 to 28 percent. The median price for a new automobile rose from \$23,000 in 2000 to \$29,500 in 2014. Consumer confidence figures made an unanticipated rise in the last two quarters of 2014 in car sales. Corporate America earned record profits in 2014, and our nearly healed economy looks very different today than it did in 2007.

The U.S. Bureau of Labor Statistics reported unemployment rates decreased to 5.5 percent in March 2015. The euro steadily rose from 88 cents on the dollar in 1997 to 1.62 in the mid-2000s. This exchange rate dropped to 1.08 euros per dollar by the end of March 2015. Oil increased from $30 to $147 per barrel in the mid-2000s, and down to $49 per barrel by March 2015; but it will increase again due to the global political and social-environmental crisis. The standard of living in Madrid, Rio de Janeiro, and other European and Latin America cites has increased for a number of years, and then decreased by 2014. The world population in 2000 was 6.1 billion. By January 2015 it had risen to 7.3 billion. A world filled with new consumers is being created, a world that will be filled with entrepreneurial opportunities.

As we continue in the second decade of the 21st century and attempt to assimilate the present political, economic and social differences, and present global crisis, we must ask ourselves: where are we today? It's clear there is no better time to step up and become an entrepreneur or intrapreneur (those who use entrepreneurial skills within an existing organization to make it more effective, efficient, and innovative). People must create their own employment opportunities. If you decide to become an entrepreneur, you must stay committed to your vision and be willing to take risks. Focus on satisfying consumers' real needs. You must give them quality, a fair price, excellent follow-up and customer service, and most importantly, innovative products and services.

Before an entrepreneur opens his or her business, s/he must know how to manage the organization. Inability to effectively manage is the number-two reason for business failure around the world (insufficient funds or financial back-up is number one). Other business killers include a lack of innovation, poor business ethics, poor sales and negotiation skills, lack of publicity, and high taxes. I have recognized these problems globally in my thirty-five years of entrepreneurial experience. Nothing is new under the sun nor have I discovered anything unknown to entrepreneurs. These same causes of business failures are corroborated by studies done in recent years by the World Bank, the Better Business Bureau, the International Economic Development Council, The Lauder Global Business Insight Report, and the Kaufman Foundation (2014).

What Do Global Entrepreneurs Have To Say?

A few entrepreneurs are well known worldwide. Most are never known outside of their neighborhoods or communities. In the last thirty years, I have conducted face-to-face interviews with over ten thousand entrepreneurs around the world and in over 140 countries who have achieved notable success in their ventures. The results of those interviews, the most important lessons I discovered in them, follow below.

Having a great idea and a business plan is easy. The real determiner of failure or success lies in distinguishing what to do next: how to get the financing, when and how to make the product and market it, and most importantly, how to persevere with your dream and continue to believe in it through the difficult economic times that persist at present. These entrepreneurs have their own circumstances, their own qualities, and their own environment and management skills. They each developed a leadership style to coincide with whatever their business demanded. The bottom line is to learn from their experiences and consider the following guidelines to become an accomplished and successful entrepreneur.

- Foster knowledge, communication, and trust. Successful entrepreneurs start with knowing about management, knowing how to convey their ideas to people, know about technology, trusting their products, and having people trust them.
- Seek opportunities. Read national and international newspapers and watch news programs, and you will see how many problems need solutions worldwide. Problems that need solving are business opportunities for entrepreneurs.
- Know your business. Choose your business and become an expert. Identify needs.
- Build your network. Work with teams. Become recognized in your industry as someone who is good at what you do.
- Use your time wisely. Don't push yourself to work seventy or eighty hours a week. Budget your time to include work, family, and friends.

- Look for what can be improved. Entrepreneurs become wealthy because they constantly offer innovations. They replace old products and provide quality service immediately.
- Be open-minded. Listen to people. Analyze and corroborate their information, but do not allow anybody to be an obstacle to your dreams.
- Entrepreneurs can make the world a better place. We create our own opportunities. We create jobs and a better standard of living for employees and their families. You are where you are because of hard work, education, trust, skills, and committed employees who work with you as a team.
- Stay with your dream. Do not let the past failures or present economic crisis make you a pessimist or make you become arrogant. Keep your dreams alive and make your community a better place to live.
- Make alliances globally and adapt to the environment.

How to Start a Successful Business

Wanting to start a business is all well and good. But there are also key steps to getting that business started.

1. Find the proper location and create a business plan.
2. Establish a corporation or other appropriate business entity according to state law to maximize tax deductions. Know the state employment rules and regulations.
3. Have money for all the initial expenses and no less than six months of working capital.
4. Secure a lease agreement, three to five years with an option for five additional years. Have an attorney review the lease contract and hire an accountant.
5. Hire a reputable construction company for the location improvements. Include a penalty clause in the contract to ensure they finish on time.
6. Obtain all the required permits and licenses
7. Obtain liability and property insurance.

Below are the most recent responses 5,536 face-to-face interviews we have done. These interviews generally lasted half an hour to forty-five minutes. We conducted these interviews with entrepreneurs who had successful small companies (with two to 135 employees and two to forty years in existence). We also include recent interviews with sixteen accountants and fifteen attorneys from Los Angeles, New York, Miami, and Latin America. We conducted the interviews with the help of MBA and B.A. students from Florida International University, Florida National University and two of the top Mexican universities accredited by the Southern Association of Colleges and Southern Universities, Tecnologico de Monterrey (ITESM) in Mexico City and the University of the Americas in Puebla, between January 2008 and February 2015. We covered cities like Anchorage, Boston, Denver, Honolulu, Juneau, Los Angeles, Miami, New Orleans, New York, Seattle, Mexico City, Montreal, Sidney, Melbourne, Mumbai, Montreal, Paris, Dubai, Cape Town, Budapest, Kathmandu, Madrid, Honk Kong, Shanghai, San Juan (Puerto Rico), Singapore, Cartagena (Colombia), Quebec, Fairfax (Canada), and over 100 countries.

What are the key factors that made your company successful?

1. Passion for offering solutions (satisfying needs).
2. Experience, education, and determination.
3. Helping clients generate more profits and value for their companies.
4. Identifying opportunities in the marketplace and working hard.
5. Building a close relationship with customers.
6. Providing post-sale support.
7. Knowing everything about your product, including costs, and having strict quality controls.
8. Being committed to your employees.
9. Teaching employees to be committed to the company.
10. Having goals and strategies and having everyone understand them.
11. Soliciting expert advice (professors, mentors, and other business people).
12. Employees understanding (precise) orders (goals); communicating.
13. Having quality products and excellent service.
14. Innovation.

What are the lessons you learned in building your company?

Business development is not a straight line. There will be highs and lows during the development of a company.

1. Always ensure your financial planning accounts for periods of time where business is slow.
2. Change if necessary. The market is constantly changing, and how you adapt to that change is the most important aspect of a business if you want to continue to grow, or survive.
3. Embrace new technology. From an operational standpoint, newer technology has made business more effective and cost efficient and allows us to enjoy better controls.
4. Cultivate a healthy corporate culture. The corporate culture of integrity and excellence established by the owner/CEO/management extends across every department and every employee associated with the company.
5. Take more risks.

What mistakes did you make during your first two years of operation?

1. Allowed the fast growth of the company to outstrip preparedness.
2. Expected all the employees to embrace the customer-oriented doctrine, and there were many mishaps.
3. Was impatient with the company's progress and did not invest enough money and resources in employees in order to enhance their development.

How do you assure your customers stay loyal to your services and products?

1. Always offer assistance and ideas to the customers.
2. Understanding that it's not all about the money. Letting the customer know that you will go the extra mile without charging him or her for everything. Adapting to your clients' needs.
3. Letting the customers know that if they call at 3:00 a.m., they will have a partner who will be there with them to solve any problem.
4. Be mobile.

What is the advice you will give to someone starting a new business?

1. Be involved with day-to-day activities. Do your research. Do solid planning and do not become too bureaucratic.
2. Understand that a business requires a lot of work, and money. You have to love it in order to stay committed to its development.
3. Connect to your industry cluster.
4. Understand that it's not all about generating profit. Profit is important, but a business is about being part of the community where you operate and serve.
5. Write detailed contracts.
6. Hire young people to bring fresh ideas to your company—integrate mobile technology into your strategy.
7. Have knowledge—go to college and learn about business, be disciplined, and be organized.
8. Do not be afraid of failure.
9. Train your personnel well and encourage them to experiment and to make decisions.
10. Get rid of people who are not committed—do not procrastinate.
11. Save for tough times.
12. Never say no to a customer.
13. Make your customer feel like a guest.

14. Keep constantly informed of market trends.
15. Do not make a customer wait.

What would you say is the single most significant challenge facing your business today?

1. Economic uncertainty.
2. Labor cost and income growth.
3. Government regulations.
4. Taxes.
5. Sales--Competition from big businesses.
6. Health care costs.
7. Ability to borrow money.

Fifteen Accountants' Responses
(Nine CPAs in the United States and Six in Latin America)
What are the key strategies an entrepreneur must use when opening a business?

1. Have base controls and procedures in place.
2. Know about your cash management: Accounts Payable/Receivable.
3. Start and build your relationship with your bank managers.
4. Use extensive scenario planning.
5. How to get further funding should the business start slow.
6. Advertise effectively.
7. Price the products/service correctly.
8. Do a cost/benefit analysis. Study the area where you want to place your business and consider costs, rent, utilities, and required permits.
9. Love what you do and take your job seriously.
10. Know your customers' needs.
11. Never compromise your integrity.

12. Have a realistic vision of where you want to take your business financially.
13. Do not go into too much debt.
14. Hire the right people.
15. Do not delegate too much.
16. Do not start a business you do not know or do not have passion for.
17. Do not wear too many hats without the expertise.

Fifteen Lawyers' Responses (Eight Attorneys from the United States, Seven in Latin America)
What are the key strategies an entrepreneur must use when opening a business?

1. If you are starting a business with a partner or partners, know what will happen if one partner leaves or dies.
2. Obtain any special licenses the business might require.
3. If the business is a franchise, know what your rights and duties are under that agreement.
4. Take any necessary steps to protect the business name or the idea regarding intellectual property.
5. Secure proper credit lines.
6. Determine market, entry, and exit strategies.
7. Check what permits you need to open your business.
8. Develop great relationships with employees, suppliers, vendors, distributors, and contractors.
9. Do marketing research.
10. Get the right people and know them well.
11. Build networks. Know how to sell yourself and the company.
12. Have the necessary capital to start a business.
13. Make time for your friends and family.
14. Get legal advice.

As I commented once while lecturing in my MBA class in Miami, "Miami, New York, Chicago, or the United States are not the center of the world, as many people think." A few of my students criticized me, but I can assure you that I am not wrong. A cohesive world force, without political self-interest, will give us better development in many countries and make life better for the world citizenry. And I am not speaking of the old idea of a world order in which some people believe that one government is in command of the globe. Never!

Former President Bill Clinton indicated in a recent world business conference in which I assisted that, "We live in an interdependent world, and in order to make it continue to work we have to have more shared prosperity... We have to assume more shared responsibilities." Yes, the world has become smaller and entrepreneurs must think globally. We must realize that we need international commerce in order to survive. Since I started teaching, I have advised my students that they had to go worldwide in order to make more opportunities for themselves and be successful. Many have followed my advice to move to the People's Republic of China and are presently living there (and other places) since the late nineties to start businesses before even graduating from college. Some of them have continued with their education in China and are presently exporting and importing. These young entrepreneurs have realized that in the last twenty years China has become one of the strongest economic powers in the world and continues to grow rapidly. These entrepreneurs strongly agree with me that China will soon be capable of dictating global economic and political policy.

> *We live in an interdependent world, and in order to make it continue to work we have to have more shared prosperity.... We have to assume more shared responsibilities.*
>
> *Bill Clinton*

China needs American food products as American economic institutions will need more Chinese investments according to the reports by the International Monetary Fund (IMF) and the Peterson Institute for International Economics (Read. *Eclipse: Living in the Shadow of China's Economic Dominance* by Arvind Subramanian, 2011). This cooperation, however, will help keep both economies built to last.

According to the World Bank (2014), China has $2.8 trillion in foreign reserves, and it's contributing over $2.3 trillion to international trade each year. As of December 2014, China owns roughly $1.4 trillion of US debts, making it America's biggest foreign investor. On the other hand, the United States is China's breadbasket. Feeding close to 1.4 billion people takes an enormous amount of resources and infrastructure. And that means tremendous business development for America as the Chinese population continues to grow. California, Florida, Iowa, and Washington sell billions of dollars of oranges, grapes, apples, soybeans, wheat, cherries, corn, and other products and raw materials to China each year. That money supports thousands of jobs, from farm fields and distribution centers to manufacturing companies. This also means more profits for us.

Many of my former students who moved to China have now become managers in multinational corporations and contact me once in a while to keep me abreast of their success, to ask for advice or to offer me a business. Others are doing business deals in Brazil, Australia, France, India, Holland, or elsewhere around the globe. I know what can happen when entrepreneurs become global. I have done it since 1987-- from New York to Mexico City, Miami to Amsterdam, Los Angeles to Buenos Aires, Rio de Janeiro, Madrid, Cape Town, Mumbai, New Delhi, Cairo, Jerusalem, Xian, Hong Kong, Shanghai, Mombasa, St Petersburg, Sydney, Perth--and everybody won. We must believe in a win-win philosophy. This is how many entrepreneurs have made our country strong globally.

Of course, I do not think that I know everything about entrepreneurship, and that I have the true and only concepts of doing business properly; there are many ways to apply your own knowledge. The stories of my entrepreneurial or management successes show how I applied my business philosophy and ethics. I delivered what I promised--always. Other stories show how I developed my character through my life experiences since a child and how I finally became who and what I am today. My style of doing business, suggestions I received from thousands of entrepreneurs around the world, and this writing will, I hope, give you food for thought so you will expand your horizons and become more conscious of the needs of other human beings.

*THE STORIES OF MY ENTREPRENEURIAL OR MANAGEMENT SUCCESSES SHOW
HOW I APPLIED MY BUSINESS PHILOSOPHY, AND ETHICS. I DELIVERED
WHAT I PROMISED, ALWAYS.*

A Nepali Entrepreneur's Vision

I met a young girl named Roji Buddhacharya in Kathmandu when she was thirteen years old. She wanted an opportunity to start exploring the international markets. She saw me attempting to converse with her mother, who spoke little English, when I purchased several handcrafted items from her small shop. Roji wanted to learn about business. My little friend wanted to sell me exquisite, meticulously crafted bronze bells that bore the special design of her religion, Buddhism. She attempted to sell me bells and many other beautiful cultural items she had in the overstocked shop. Apparently she had noticed that I had a great deal of interest in the bells, and that caught her attention—she

knew I was a sure sale. She came from a family of five and was the oldest of the siblings.

I had been observing Roji for a while and saw how well she handled her negotiations with other business people and tourists. Though young, she was very enthusiastic. This enthusiasm allowed her to persuade anybody who approached her to purchase a five- or ten-dollar item. She quickly impressed me with her attitude and the persistence with which she sold her products in broken English. I finally purchased several handcrafted bells from her. I informed her that I was interested in purchasing more bells, but I did not need them until I returned to America to see if I could find a market. I said that once I was ready, I was going to email her and make a wire transfer for the products. Two months later, after I had returned home, a UPS employee delivered a box with ten bells, necklaces, and several other handcrafted items from Nepal. Accompanying the items was a letter from my little friend saying that she had sent the items on consignment.

Young Roji's visionary thinking, self-confidence, forthright attitude, and service-oriented manner of conducting business are common qualities possessed by entrepreneurs worldwide. She wanted to start saving money for college in California, and I was willing to participate in her goal. It is obvious my enthusiastic partner had the heart of an entrepreneur. After we shook hands, she said, "Remember that I am a little girl but with a big business heart." She took a big risk because she had a specific goal. She was willing to go forward with this opportunity to export to America and seized the moment when the opportunity arrived. Before receiving her first payment, she had forwarded me, via the Internet, over five hundred photographs of all the handcrafted items she could sell me. She had also researched the most cost-effective way to send more products to America and was ready to start shipping. She had a vision.

"I AM A LITTLE GIRL BUT WITH A BIG BUSINESS HEART."

CHAPTER 9

Working with the Poor

———————•◆•———————

Poverty is perhaps the most serious threat to world peace,
even more dangerous than terrorism, religious fundamentalism,
ethnic hatred, political rivalries, or any of the other forces that are often cited
as promoting violence and war. Poverty leads to hopelessness,
which provokes people to desperate acts.

Muhammad Yunus

Successfully working with the poor requires that a person be humble, respectful, and motivated by love, not by pity. I became involved in the quest to fight poverty as the result of a lifetime promise I had made in my younger years. I had something substantial to offer, something more than handouts, and I felt that I could help the economically disadvantaged make lasting changes in their lives so they could eventually better themselves instead of having to rely on someone else.

I started traveling back and forth between the United States and Latin America in late 1982. My traveling led me across the paths of many indigent people who needed help. Meeting so many poor people touched my heart and caused me to thank God for my good life, for what he had given me. I started helping the poor by giving them money so they could buy food or medication for their children. Fathers and mothers approached me in the streets because they needed me to buy medication for their sick children, whom they carried in their arms as proof. I was naïve, and I was deceived. I learned that those parents did not use the money I had given them for its intended purpose. They were asking (or drugged) their children to play sick so that they would have money to indulge in liquor or gambling. Vice is the most common disease there, and everywhere. It's also contagious, a fact that became apparent to me as I saw what some government and private organization officials were doing as the fiscal year was coming to an end and they had budget surpluses. The leaders had to spend the entire budget, regardless of how unnecessary the expenditure might have been, so that the following year's budget would not be smaller.

Top non-governmental organizations (NGOs) or non-profit organization managers often follow the same procedure. They claim to be saving pennies, while at the same time they are wasteful and spend excessive amounts on super-fluous items. This means that a high percentage of the funds donated to an NGO might be used to cover administrative costs or to pay for foolish expen-ditures like expensive laptops and extensive, unnecessary travel and hotel expen-ditures for meetings, when Internet communication could be utilized instead. In this manner the wholehearted purpose of the donation is lost because only 30 to 65 percent of those donations go toward the purpose for which it was originally intended in many cases.

We must hold the presidents, CEOs, and administrators accountable when they present manicured reports about operating budgets instead of reports about what their charitable organizations have accomplished. We have already seen the pernicious results of misleading, manicured reports in the Washington

Mutual bankruptcy (2010), the Bernie Madoff scandal (2009), the General Service Administration (GSA) scandal and indictment in Las Vegas (2014, 2010), Bank of America (2012), the Barclays Bank in London, and other banks worldwide, over the manipulation of interest rates affecting trillions of dollars globally which has inflamed an already angry public toward these type of unscrupulous actions in the last five years.

I changed my strategy. Instead of giving the little money I had to help the poor, I decided to purchase the medication or food for their families and the raw materials or equipment they needed in order to start a micro business, with no interest. To elaborate, I might meet an indigent laborer who knew about basket weaving but did not have the cash to buy the materials to make the quantity of products necessary to make a profit. So I would help her purchase the materials. Another example would be a seamstress who was working as a maid and could double or triple her salary by sewing or making dresses but did not have a sewing machine, an expensive item in Latin America. I would purchase the sewing machine for her. Additionally, I would teach the poor about negotiations when buying raw materials or other equipment, and the principles of managing their micro business. Most small business owners do not have an understanding of these principles, and their businesses fail. Eighty percent of small businesses in Latin America fail within the first two years.

I have a great deal of respect for the poor. I found they while they had talent to make their own products and cultivate their land, what they lacked was the know-how to manage their products in a business environment. I wanted to teach them to manage their businesses efficiently so they could take care of their own endeavors, create employment opportunities for themselves or friends, and provide for their families without having to leave their country as so many had done between 1990 and 2010 (see the *Migration Policy Institute report*, 2004. *Immigrants and Homeownership in Urban America: An Examination of Nativity, Socio-Economic and Place*).

According to the PEW Hispanic Center, a nonpartisan, nonprofit research organization in Washington D.C., and the Mexican government's National Institute of Statistics, Information and Geography Bureau (INEGI), from

2005-2010 an average of three hundred thousand immigrants left Mexico every year to come to the United States illegally, dropping substantially in 2011-12. About 11.2 illegal immigrants from various countries were living in the United States according to a report published by PEW in January 2012. According to a news story posted online by the Round Rock Leader on August 31, 2013, Rep. John Carter, indicated, "The reality is that about 40 percent of the people came in on an airplane, with a legal visa, and just overstayed their visa and have never gone home." Illegal immigration is a serious and costly issue globally, and it is a problem that must be handled expeditiously worldwide for the protection of family unity and social progress.

As of the beginning of 2012, Mexico's National Institute of Immigration (INM) and the National Security Council estimated that over one-hundred and fifty thousand people per year cross the southern border unlawfully into Mexico, while civil-society organizations mentioned that number over three-hundred thousand. Ninety percent of these immigrants come from El Salvador, Guatemala, Honduras, and Nicaragua. These people leave Central America yearly in an attempt to come to the U.S. searching for "The American Dream".

Jennifer Dresel (2012, January 23) who writes for the Heinrich Boll Stiftung Foundation, North America, indicates in her article *"Dangerous Journey. Migration through the transient land Mexico,"* and Paloma Esquivel (2012, April 8) of the *Los Angeles Times*, corroborated in her article *"Making the border less enticing to cross,"* and Mark Stevenson's article again reiterated (2014, April 9) in the Associated Press, *"Honduras Migrants Request Mexico to Allow Free Passage,"* what immigrants from Central America have to face:

In August 2011, seventy-two illegal migrants were killed in the northern state of Tamaulipas and this tragic event accelerated and enhanced public awareness to the problem of severe human rights violations toward Central American migrants in Mexico, and new cases are continually coming out in the open. The majority of the migrants killed in Mexico are never identified and remain nameless, and more people are dying in the attempt to come to the United States of America. The migration flow coming through Mexico and heading toward America constitutes the largest in the world. . .Mexico is a transit as well as target country for migrants from Central America, in addition to itself being a source country of emigrants. It is also a commonplace for migrants…to be mistreated, lied to, blackmailed, robbed, and physically attacked by corrupt police and migration officials. Furthermore, the violence has proliferated even more with extortions, kidnappings, torture, rapes of women and murders committed by armed criminal gangs. Many of these atrocities are carried out in collaboration with the local authorities. Violent crime has also soared with the increasing participation of the drug cartels in people smuggling, which in recent years has proven to be a particularly lucrative and less risky source of income than the drug trade. According to the report "The Globalization of Crime" by the United Nations Office on Drugs and Crime (2010, June 17), transnational criminal alliances such as Los Zetas, the Gulf Cartel, are strongly involved in migrant smuggling.

Ken Ellingwood (2012, May 6) reported in his article in the *Los Angeles Times*, *"Mexican shelter is at a crossroads,"* as he writes what a Central American migrant worker says who is attempting to reach U.S. and points at different routes to take, "…all roads lead to trouble. Up here, kidnappers and drug killers. Over there, Mexican army checkpoints. Farther along, a giant dessert, with poisonous snakes and deadly heat…." The poor have no alternatives and they have to migrate, as they have no opportunities in their countries. The poor are proud people who do not want anybody to give them anything for free. What the poor want is employment, and they want to be educated. They want to work and earn their own money so they may purchase necessities. They are honest, hardworking people who want to be respected.

There have been times when I have been volunteering with different NGOs or the church, or working alone on a variety of jobs such as creating water drainage systems or building roads, and village leaders would often tell me that they did not want what we had to offer them. They had lived in their customary manner for long generations, since the time before the Spanish conquered their ancestors. "We respect our traditions," they said. "Our traditions involve living with nature and the way mother earth has provided for us." Yes, they want to be assisted, "we want to create jobs; we want to create opportunities, we want to be productive here at home so our children do not leave." The poor do not want unearned gifts.

A common problem throughout Latin America is a lack of support in creating opportunities, a lack of business knowledge or management by most micro and small-business owners. A family of three tills the land and grows corn by buying the seed, fertilizer, and other products needed to grow their product, on credit. Once the harvest is done, they sell the product, and their profit, they think, is $800. They also have enough corn in their warehouse to last for a few months. This seems acceptable on the surface. The problem these families have is that they have never seen $800 at one time; it's an extraordinary amount to them. When someone makes an offer for their corn, they think that they have made a profit, and they have, but it's rarely as much as they could have earned. The cost to produce that corn was three or four times more than their profit. They did not factor in their operational costs. They should have sold the corn for $5,000 or more. The poor do not suffer from stupidity; they suffer from government support, or political and bureaucratic corruption affecting the quality of public policy.

The poor in Latin America have been taken advantage of for centuries by government, the private sector, and multinational business representatives. These centuries of mistrust lead them to view any newcomers skeptically, as shown in Eduardo Galeano's (1971) *The Open Veins of Latin America* and Alan Riding's (1989) *Distant Neighbor: A Portrait of the Mexicans.* You have to earn the privilege to be with them if you want to be a volunteer in their villages. You cannot just show up wherever they live and dictate the terms of the relationship. You may think that you know it all and act arrogant since you have economic means or a doctorate, or have received top honors in your field of endeavor. These things mean nothing to them. They can see through you. They can tell if you are sincere and genuine in wanting to assist them or if you are fake and a hypocrite. You must be humble; in due course they will respect you. The poor can contribute to world development by sharing their rich cultural values and histories. An unknown American writer said this best:

Economic power is measured not only by what it produces, but by how it touches human lives. Consequently, economic decisions have human consequences and moral content; they help or hurt people, strengthen or weaken family lives, advance or diminish the quality of justice in our land. It is important that we use the resources of our own faith, the strength of our economy, and the opportunities of our democracy to shape a society that better protects the dignity and basic rights of other human beings both in our country and worldwide.

I volunteered to give therapeutic massages to poor children with epilepsy and muscular dystrophy. I washed floors and cleaned the whirlpools in the *Centro de Rehabilitacion Infantil* in Cuernavaca (CRIC) (Infantile Rehabilitation Center, Cuernavaca). The hospital only had two maintenance ladies. They could not keep the premises clean by themselves, so I helped them when I was not busy. Libertad Ocaña, a sixty-five-year-old Spanish nurse, had served as the center's director for over thirty years. She had a remarkable love for all the children who came to her center. I met her after donating medicine to the hospital.

The president of CRIC's board of directors wanted to meet me. He was interested in having me join the board. I was not interested in becoming a board member; I only wanted to help the children at this shorthanded hospital. I was committed to assisting the children in therapy sessions. I also set up product-raising drives wherein we asked Pond's (now known as Unilever) and other companies to donate top-quality products that were unsalable due to damaged boxes. After receiving these donations, we would sell them on our own, with the proceeds going to cover expenses at the center. I continued to act as the center's representative for years and constantly solicited donations wherever I was.

The Peanut Bag Kids

Another project that I set up involved homeless street children in Mexico City. While teaching at the Tec de Monterrey Mexico City campus in 1995, I had seen several kids, aged ten to twelve years old, selling bags of peanuts. Every time they ran out of peanuts, they had to take a taxi or the local bus to go buy more peanut bags. They wasted time because they spent two or three hours a day buying their products. Worse, they were missing school. I spoke to them several times. I told them I would act as their business partner on the condition that they follow my rules. They agreed. I asked them to find out the price of a large box of peanuts and loaned them $100.00 to purchase a thousand peanut bags. We got a better price due to the volume we were buying. At the end of each week, the profits were distributed evenly between

the children and me. However, I told them that I would give them my share of the profits as an extra bonus if they met the following points:

1. They must go to school every day.
2. To be part of the team, each child had to maintain at least a C+ average. Those who maintained a B average received an extra ten dollars.
3. Each member had to take a bath at least three times a week and show up to work clean.
4. There would be no lying or stealing of any kind.
5. We would work as a team.

This program lasted nine years. Between 1995 and 2006, our team grew to about a hundred children between the ages of twelve and fourteen, working at three different universities. The proceeds of my share were used to buy them school uniforms and personal items they needed. Six kids went on to college through the program.

The Homeless in Manhattan

There is no such thing as a typical homeless person. Many of the people I met at Central Park in New York since 1998 had been incredibly successful earlier in their lives. There was John; he was seventy-eight. His fame led to an involvement with drugs. Eventually he transformed into an alcoholic. He lost his job, his family, and everything he had earned.

There was Frank. He and I shared a meal occasionally. Sometimes he would disappear for several weeks only to reappear in his familiar spot at 'The Pond" in Central Park. I would spot him from my apartment on Central Park South overlooking the park, walking casually with his girlfriend. Whenever we met, he would say, "Hello, Michael, sorry I couldn't come to see you, but I've been busy with my girlfriend who is having a drug problem." She was a former salesperson from New Jersey. Michael was about sixty-four. He had given thirty years of his life to Macy's before being laid off during the 1990s recession. He had lost his family soon thereafter and was moving between various shelter homes from New Jersey to Manhattan. Like many others, he slept on the front steps of either Saint Thomas Episcopal Church on Fifth Avenue and Fifty-Third or the Fifth Avenue Presbyterian Church. He was a quiet, lonely man with a tragic and mundane history.

There was Eloise, aged forty-six, and a kind lady with a constant smile whether it was a cold, snowy day, or a hot summer night. Eloise loved to talk about anything and everything. She had been a prominent marketing manager in Manhattan for over twenty-five years. Her philosophy about life was that a person could do what he or she wanted as long as nobody was deceived. She damaged her mind by taking too many drugs in her younger years. Often I would find her picking leftovers out of different restaurant trash bags in the business district. She separated her food into different plastic bags that she organized neatly in an old leather handbag. She had one bag for each meal of the day. Sometimes she would walk into the park or get lost somewhere in the subway tunnel adjacent to the Plaza Hotel. One day in spring, she told me that she was moving from the area to Baltimore, where she had friends and family. Her friend was going to give her a ride. She asked me for a small loan. I was happy to oblige her. A few weeks later, I received a postcard from her that read, "Thank you for listening to me."

Volunteering for the Catholic Church in Latin America and at St. Paul the Apostle's Church in Manhattan has been an eye-opening experience. I have worked on diverse charitable projects for the church, such as assisting the poor with basic necessities, building churches or a seminary, investing, providing for the elderly, helping to provide meals, or at the very least, providing company for the homeless at St. Paul's.

The Catholic Church performs countless noble deeds globally, but the clergy does not want to be mentioned. They are humble men. Working with the clergy since the early 1980s has been a rewarding experience. I am well aware that there have been grave errors committed by a few priests who must be held accountable for their actions, but it should not be forgotten that there are over four hundred thousand other clergymen in the world who are deeply committed to giving their lives unselfishly.

In 2004, I was involved in researching and helped establish the 2006–2010 strategic planning platform for World Vision International (WVI), a global charitable organization. The area I was responsible for included Latin America and the Caribbean. WVI ran a number of outstanding programs, but it lacked organization in a few areas, and there was distrust and jealousy between the WVI presidents of different countries. To increase its effectiveness, WVI had to work to make the organization more efficient and effective in other countries in Latin America. This would involve a policy of information sharing between programs in different countries as opposed to each program zealously defending its own territory at the cost of others. It should not be forgotten that NGOs like WVI are working to help the poor. The more efficient and organized their systems are, the more cost effective they will become, and, ultimately, the more people in need are benefited.

At a World Vision conference in Colorado Springs, Colorado, I witnessed in an unfortunate statement made by the outgoing president of the international NGO in 2009. In his farewell speech, he stated, "I am very proud to have traveled five million miles around the world and to have met important people in the last ten years." Several people at my table looked upset. I knew what they were thinking because I was thinking the same thing. I refused to keep quiet. I said, loudly, "Where did he get the money to pay for all those airplane tickets?" A high-ranking official who worked for the same NGO as the man giving the speech looked at me carefully. After a few seconds of silence, she responded, "You're right. I was thinking the same thing. He should be ashamed of himself."

I have seen thousands of children go to bed hungry; the money for those tickets, purchased with donated money, could have given those children food for months. That wasted money could have purchased medicine and other basic necessities. This is why many donors have stopped giving money to help some non-profit organizations. They see that we have people whose reasons for getting involved are not entirely altruistic.

There Will Always Be Thieves

I had been investing my life's earnings for a several years to help the poor. I wanted to set up an NGO where the smallest possible percentage of money would go to administrative costs. A more conscious management strategy was called for. I had been a volunteer and a member of the board with several small and international organizations in the last thirty years. My experience and commitment had taught me how to create such an organization. Unfortunately fraud got in the way of my plans. I was getting ready to withdraw my investment from a Mexican firm I had invested with for several years. This was in April 2008. When I asked to receive my money, the company's president and founder began to vacillate and would not deposit the amounts I requested.

I visited their headquarters in Monterrey, Mexico, and met several times with the company's president. He promised that he would return my funds within eight months. In late 2009, the company's employees disappeared, although I was able to speak to the president twice that year. He assured me that nothing was wrong. HRN Mexico Corporation (a fictitious name) was affiliated with a company in New York.

In 2010, I found the New York office in the Empire State Building and after interviewing two young recent college graduate employees; I learned that the owners were doing illegal financial movements. The president and his two sons at HRN stole my money and destroyed the dreams of many people. But of course this occurred because I had allowed greed to come into my mind. I made a mistake by not listening to my heart and did not follow the old Chinese saying, "Do not mistake temptation for opportunity."

These people went underground and are presently running from the law. The last I heard, Interpol had detected them in Spain; but finally, one of the sons was arrested in Mexico City in August of 2010 and was facing trial, but strangely, according to my attorney a judge released him in late 2012. A second son was arrested in 2014 and is presently in prison facing legal proceedings. It is obvious that these people are protected. The money is gone. In spite of this great setback, I have not allowed my work with the poor to be derailed. I have continued to help them however I can.

As if 2009 had not been trying enough, I was "express kidnapped" (as it is termed in Mexico) by three plainclothes police officers in Mexico City. I had flown in from Miami the previous night and was heading to a board of directors meeting at World Vision Mexico. It was still dark, about fifteen minutes before sunrise, and the street was busy with food vendors, people going to work, and medical students. While en route to the WV building, the driver took a wrong turn. I brought it to his attention, and he responded that he had made a mistake. A few moments later, he stopped, and two armed men with pistols got into the cab. One of the men who got in the back seat with me immediately began to strike my ribs with his elbow. He continuously hit me for about an hour as I was being driven around the north end of Mexico City. He took my pen from my shirt pocket and used it to almost gouge my left eye out of its socket. The subjects took all my belongings, including my clothing. My ribs hurt badly; I was in pain. I asked them to let me go after they had taken my property. I told them I was a humanitarian doing volunteer work for WV and I had a meeting to attend. The man sitting in the front seat told me he knew about WV. He told me that I wouldn't have to worry about the meeting because I was a dead man--I would be killed because I had seen his face.

After I had endured a terrible eternity during which my life was in the balance, the cab stopped and the subject sitting in the back seat with me told me to get out of the car. He had seen the photos I was carrying in my briefcase. They were of indigent people my organization and I were helping around the globe. The pictures and my talking possibly touched his heart and persuaded him to spare me. As I was sliding to his side to get out of the cab, he whispered in my left ear. "Keep on walking straight and please do not look back." I walked away uncertainly, on edge. I was waiting for a bullet to penetrate my back or possibly my head. I prayed. I then heard the man who had let me out of the car yell "No!" and heard a thud. The vehicle sped away. I kept on walking. Eventually a lady in her late seventies came to my assistance when she saw me semi-naked and stumbling on the sidewalk. She dressed me. I felt relief and thanked God, for allowing me to continue with my life and be able to see my family again.

When I called the police department, the watch commander said, "It would be best to keep quiet and not to make a report because the robbers know where you live and terrible things could happen to your family." I arrived at the Word Vision offices at about 8:30 a.m. and resigned. I let the other directors know that I felt it was too risky to travel in Mexico City, at least for the immediate future. I was born again on that particular day when I came so close to dying— July 13, 2009.

That's life—filled with surprises, and while not all of them have been pleasant, I realize how fortunate I am to be living my dream. I have endeavored to share my dream with others, to make them part of the great fortune I have experienced, although it has certainly been hard at times. God has given me many blessings, and I have maintained the attitude that whenever I engage myself in any endeavor, I know from the very first moment that it is going to be successful. I have always acted on the assumption that nothing will go wrong with my plans and that even if problems do arise, they will take care of themselves, and continue. However, you really have to be ready academically, spiritually, and never stop learning, as it entails hard work, and dedication.

I admit that I have met negative and bigoted individuals.

Far more memorably, and far more importantly, I have met many beautiful and kind people along the path my life has taken. There have been many good times and few bad times, but during all these years, I have listened to the music of my heart and allowed my life to follow where it has led. As it stands right now, I would not have done anything differently or changed a think.

And as I reflect on the circumstances and events that have brought me to today, I can't help but think anything other than my life...what a life!

www.ingramcontent.com/pod-product-compliance
Lightning Source LLC
Chambersburg PA
CBHW020424290526
45785CB00002B/713